HOW THE MIND WORKS

HOW THE MIND WORKS

Understanding human thoughts and behaviors

Carlo Lazzari

iUniverse, Inc.
New York Lincoln Shanghai

How The Mind Works
Understanding human thoughts and behaviors

iUniverse books may be ordered through booksellers or by contacting:

iUniverse
2021 Pine Lake Road, Suite 100
Lincoln, NE 68512
www.iuniverse.com
1-800-Authors (1-800-288-4677)

The views expressed in this work are solely those of the author and do not necessarily reflect the views of the publisher, and the publisher hereby disclaims any responsibility for them.

ISBN: 978-0-595-45132-6 (pbk)
ISBN: 978-0-595-89444-4 (ebk)

Printed in the United States of America

Index

1   Introduction

1.1. Introduction

Thinking helps us to survive. Life would be impossible without the use of our thinking to solve simple or complex problems. It is natural to think. In fact, we do it without excessive efforts, except when we have to solve difficult problems. Other times, emotions, anxiety, lack of concentration play an important role in impeding thinking. The link between thinking and emotions is strong and it is hard to believe that there could be such a pure thought that is not affected by our emotional status in a given moment. Nevertheless, thinking is so basic in our profession that a slight influence by other mental processes could jeopardize the life of people who depend on that person. If a bus driver makes the wrong evaluation of a signal because is emotionally distracted by mental images of his boss who has announced him that he will be fired next week, the life of all passengers is at risk. We also know that "drinking and driving" is not the right choice if we are driving our cars and must "clearly evaluate the road that takes us from a party to our home". Even slight emotional "jerks" that come from our brain, and are part of our life, somehow send a signal to that part of our brain that is involved in a process of thinking. At this point, we need a definition of thinking that is closer to what it is usually meant in this book. First of all, I refer to all processes of problem-solving. *Mainly, thinking is any activity of our brain in reading, ordering, and manipulating data in order to solve problems.* With the aim of making things easier to be visualized, I used many drawings and simple mathematical expressions just to synthesize the concepts expressed about thinking. In many parts of the book, I have also used logic expressions and symbols. But I kept them at a simple level, and with the specific aim to reach some of the goals of this book. One objective was to simplify the way of expressing the dynamics of human thinking by using simple mathematical models, to grasp a complex process. This would help us to have a "key" which we can use whenever we refer to that process. Explaining the process of thinking through logics and algebraic expressions may help to see how our mental processes very much resemble many other actions in our life. It is like saying that in our daily life, in our activities, in our emotional turmoil or preoccupation, we can identify some basic processes, which have common roots in the way we apply problem-solving. In addition, we will see mental operations that generate emotions. This is like exploring the origin of our ideas, thoughts, behaviors, and personality.

2 Exploring mind and its wonders

2.1. Starting to "open" our mind

Many philosophical, mathematical, and neurobiological scientists have tried to underline the importance of mind in human life and thinking. No matter what the interpretative paradigm for studying mind was, some extraordinary papers have been written about how our mind works. Even today, there is a fascination in reading what is daily found about the way our mind works. Before offering a historical view of mind studies, I would like to make a distinction between what is brain and what is mind. Perhaps, it can be simplified by thinking to our car. It is pushed by a motor which is the brain of the car. However, whatever a car is able to do on the road, its "functioning", its behavior on the way, is determined by the whole engine work. Two engines may look similar, they belong to the same car, they have been constructed by the same company, but practically, they do not work the same way. One engine seems better than the other. Functionally they seem being two different souls. Mind is more or less the same thing. It is the way our brains function. It is the operative section of our brain. Structurally we cannot identify mind or where different functions and activities take place. We can do this with our brain. We can study our brain with PET, TAC or other diagnostic instruments. But when we are asked to localize where our thoughts take place, where is the centre for categorical thinking or the centre for mistaken thoughts, we have no instruments that say: "It takes place in that part of the brain". For the whole book, I will be talking about the many activities that our brain performs. The work it does and how well it does it. However, the models I have created are empirical and predict some way our neurons work, but not where all this activity takes place. In other words I will talk about how the car moves and behaves on the road. But no mention is done on the individual parts of the engine. I will also make simple examples to illustrate how different mental mechanisms will act.

2.2. Philosophy of mind

There are many scientific articles that have been written about mind. However, I found that the discipline that most treats mind and its function at the same time are Cybernetics and Logics. This has historically been the first philosophical-biological approach to mind functions, before the explosion of modern neurophysiology and neuro-anatomy. However, some concepts of Cybernetics that have helped modern robotics and informatics sciences still deserve attention because they help to explain complex activities by using simple examples. Moreover, also with modern neurophysiology it is valuable to make a clear distinction between what is brain function (i.e., long term and short memory, dreaming, earring, seeing, emotions, etc.) and what is a mind function (i.e., thinking, abstract thought, problem-solving, predicting, etc.). Mind functions are often refereed as cognitive activities. In this book, I will also use some simple mathematic expressions trying to link concepts that are shared amongst several sciences: neuro-anatomy and neurophysiology, cognition, formal logics, cybernetics, etc.

One thing that our mind is able to do with some degree of perfection is thinking. All our life is dedicated to problem-solving. This mainly is the "work" that our mind does. Even when we are not apparently solving problems, and are painting or playing a tune, we are involved in some sort of problem-solving. This requires some basic steps that our mind is asked to perform, such as recognizing the nature of the problem, and collecting information for its solution. Some problems are more complex than others, and sometimes they take all our life for their solutions. Other times, some events that surround us make thinking more difficult, like the noise of a road, or the heat in a room. "Disturbing" factors can be internal, such as our emotions that can aid thinking (like positive emotions) or hinder it (like depression or anxiety).

A thought process, that is, what we do for solving problems, can last minutes or years. A thought process is complete when we have the solution to the problem we are examining, while for more complex tasks, thought processes go on for years, other problems are never solved[1]. One way we have to check if we are on the right way is via some sort of information called "feed-backs". Actually, there are two kinds of feedbacks: positive, that maintains the activity of our mind (a sort of: "OK, go on!") and negative that inhibits the thought process (a sort of: "Stop there! It's not the right solution! Try another thing!"). Daily, we are submersed by feedbacks, although we are not aware of these messages. They are part of our life, and, of our thinking. This suggests that we are not aware or "conscious" about a lot of events happening in our mind.

Consciousness is not always related to thinking, and many thought processes are not always linked to a complete consciousness of mind. For example, many automatisms belong to categories of thinking with a low awareness. When we drive a car almost any action is automatic allowing us to focus our attention on the traffic and on the road conditions. If I try to express this by using some symbols, I would say:

1. If x is the problem I want to solve by thinking,
2. and if τ is thought process that helps me to solve x,
3. and if τx represent the whole process of using my mind to solve a problem,
4. then, I cannot be always aware of τx or thought process, although I can clearly identify what the problem is. Some solutions come automatically in our mind! And smartness is a characteristic of all human beings.

I can represent consciousness with the symbol C, while the awareness of the thought process with $C\tau x$. When I am driving my car, and I see a child suddenly crossing the road, my foot automatically presses the brake pedal, in a second, without being conscious of the in-between thought processes:

1. "A child is crossing the road!".
2. "If you do not stop immediately you can harm that child!".
3. "You have no time to modify your route!".
4. "Brake pedal is under your right/left foot!".
5. "Please activate the muscle of your foot to apply the right strength to your foot!".
6. "Finally, break!".

Six steps without hesitation! A real record of our mind. Before closing this chapter I would like to recall some words of two eminent philosophers: "Thus we reach the widely popular view that mind is encased in a non-mental and impenetrable shell, within which it may cherish the secrets of its own essence without being disturbed by the inquisitive intruders"[2].

What enchants us most about mind are its complexity and secretes. However, we can discover the secrets of the objective world by simply examining under a magnifying lens the processes that our mind uses to register what is in the objective world. In a certain sense, we reflect these mind processes by the way we behave, talk, perform or do things. Whatever we express by way of words, actions, behaviors, is an expression of operations performed in our mind. No matter how simple or creative our expressions can be. What we express (by words or behaviors) is always a template or trace of our mind operations. There is a flip flop process between world-mind-world. The objective world is registered and mastered by our mind. Then, we understand our mind processes by observing what we create symbolically or practically. These are the footprints of our thought processes. Therefore "the individual mind is regarded as a functional order expressing in conscious form the structural principle of the universe"[3].

In the universe of mind processes, there are also abstract concepts, metaphors, and dreams. In a research I made in people with mild cerebral dementia, dreams had a vivid characteristic, and were often confused with reality. These subjects seemed loosing their power to differentiate reality from dream. I named this aspect with "dreamphrenia" to recall schizophrenia where a similar confusion between self and reality can occur[4][5][6]. This would suggest that richness in though process is not only a matter of complexity of mental operations. Rather we need also a reality test, that is, we should know where our mental processes, dreams, creations, fantasies are, and where we are. If we believe to be really in the Magic World of Oz, perhaps we need to make some appointment with our analyst. If we believe that real world shares something in common with the Magic World of Oz, we can write an article for some newspaper. We always need to locate our mental processes. Thinking cannot happen in a vacuum, and it needs to stick to reality and to a sane reality test.

One way of disclosing ideas to others is through the use of language. My words, the way I express my thoughts, feelings, concepts, and ideas are "revealed" by my words. However, there are distracted listeners, and others that can make fine discriminations in my thoughts. A psychologist or a specialist in communication can say a lot about thought processes, but not everything. Therefore, when I tell you what is in my mind, I do this by words; but you know my words and not exactly what is in my mind; "you know my mind only after and through hearing my words"[7]. And if I apply some decoding grid to your words, I can approximate the understanding of your mental processes. In other words, I can hypothesize what mental and logical processes you are applying when you say: "People are always the same!". An example. In this expression there is a sort of generalization. Apart from the tone of voice, I can suspect that the category "people" is linked to "same" although a reference is missing: "The same to whom?". The information is incomplete, but clear enough to be classified as a sort of generalization. Here the category "Same" or "S" is the set which includes all people, p_1, p_2, p_3, p_n. A first classification of this code with the use of set theory is: $S = \{p_1, p_2, p_3, p_n\}$. Those who are familiar with cognitive psychology know that generalization can be found in some circumstances, like depression. In this book, we will also learn how to code words in order to "unveil secret thoughts". The result is that the statement "People are always the same" is a generalization where different categories or information are attributed to the same superset or code. This process is common in a state of fatigue (depression is a sort of psychic fatigue), tiredness, rage or worry. Functionally, mind is overwhelmed by emotions to the detriment of fine discrimination because "people are not always the same, and people are different from each other".

2.3. Making inferences about mind processes

In a certain way, our mind treats inputs or outputs from environment by using some form of mathematical or logic operation. For example, in the expression "3 + 2 = 5" the numbers 3 and 2 represent the inputs while 5 is the output, which is the conclusion of our mind. The sign "+" is indeed the way in which our mind elaborates the inputs 3 and 2. For example, when I ask to the vendor "I want 3 hotdogs plus 2 hotdogs", and he replies "So, you want 5 hotdogs", his mind is working better than mine because he is not hungry as I am. More or less, all our minds can elaborate inputs in an infinite number of ways. For example as "3 × 2", "3 – 2", "3 ÷ 2", etc.

In each case, the output will change, being respectively, "6", "1", "1.5", etc. However, some other predictions could also be made. By knowing that the output is 5 we could predict any input if we know how our mind is working (if it *sums* inputs, if it *multiplies* inputs, if it *divides* inputs, or if it *subtracts* inputs).

Usually, what happens in psychological and social sciences is that at the beginning we know the output: for example depression, aggressive act, and suicide of a client in a counseling service. Then, we investigate family and personal history, social traumas, social relationships of that person, peer influence, etc. Finally, we arrive to a conclusion on how clients' mind is actually working: for instance, if s/he has developed a depressed way of elaborating world inputs, then is *multiplying* his/her difficulties, and is *subtracting* from his repertoire useful coping strategies to face life events. Therefore, by just using mathematical operations, if two life events, in the recent life of this client, are indicated as A (loss of a parent) and B (being fired), from the output reactions we make inferences about how his/her mind is reacting to losses. Let us say that the reaction (output) is C: becoming depressed. In some instances, by knowing the magnitude of C, depression, during counseling we investigate if some loss occurred. That is, the counselor asks to this client if A and/or B have occurred. The counselor starts from the assumption that this person('s mind) has elaborated inputs A and B by "summing them up". But if the reaction is C' (e.g., suicide) probably s/he has reacted in a disproportionate manner to A and B. S/he has not summed the inputs, neither has s/he subtracted them. S/he has simply "multiplied" the magnitude of these losses and the effects.

This way of making inferences about inputs (life events, stresses, daily deeds, etc.) when the output is known makes the basis of psychological diagnosis.

Anyway, systems inference is very important also when we deal with social events. In this case, the process of inference is even more complex but the process of deducing inputs by starting from outputs is what we usually call as "looking for causes". Causes are inputs, while effects are outputs. Social scientists like to make inferences on how social systems (psychological, social, and anthropological) elaborate inputs (respectively, life events, historical and social changes, cultural happenings).

If A is a state of affective deprivation, and B a state of family crisis, the output C, depression, could be predicted by knowing how other people usually react in similar circumstances. However, by definition, men and their minds are not predictable, and what are right to make are only plausible hypotheses. Mind can adapt to stressful events: a) with no effort ($A + B = 0$) (with 0 being the magnitude adjustment in our emotional mind); b) with a minimal change ($A + B \geq 0$); or c) with unpredictable and disastrous thought processes ($A + B = \infty$).

When I visit a patient because he has some crises, I have already the output: mind is reacting with ideas that are verbally expressed by that person in crisis. From here on, my intervention depends on my theoretical framework. By knowing exactly the inputs, I can bring them into a conscious awareness (e.g., psychoanalytic approach): "You have problems with your Super-Ego borrowed by your parents". I can also work on coping strategies in order to change the way in which that person's mind reacts to environment without paying much attention to past experiences (inputs): and this is the counseling approach: "You have already gone through all this in your past. What do you remember you have done to cope with it?". Or by using some integrated approach. Cognitive approaches are very much interested in how mind actually elaborates inputs form the inner-emotional or outer-physical world. Is that person "summing" or "multiplying" the inputs from his/her environment? How can we treat him in order to promote a more adaptive behavior? That is, what kind of interventions should be made in order to switch his or her emotional mind into a different order of elaborating inputs? Psychotherapy acts by changing the logic of basic assumptions: that is by mirroring to the client how his mental constructions sound like. Psycho-diagnosis and all psychological tests make inferences on how mind works. Both are essentials for an integrated model. In any case, mind elaborates inputs form the inner-emotional and outer-physical world in some way which should be reduced into simple models. In this book, formal logic or mathematical transformations are used to predict the way in which mind is functioning.

2.4. States of mind alertness

We all are familiar with the fact that our mind does not like to work when we are at the end of a tiring work day. Much less inclined to form complex thoughts if we are awaken during our night sleep. To arrive to people under total anesthesia who form only simple and rudimentary ideas. Therefore, our mind goes through several states of alertness. Sometimes, it works in a brilliant manner. Other times, we have the impression that it goes very slowly. In extreme instances, our mind is off. If I say a word to my friend but he has an earphone or is sleeping, very likely he could not hear my words. Saying it in cybernetic words, whatever the inputs are, the system mind does not give signs of receiving them; it cannot be alerted by feedbacks coming from environment, neither from signals deriving from inner emotional states. In my friend, there are no reactions to my words, at least on a conscious level. In order to identify activated or quiescent minds we can introduce a shorthand indicating with the sign "+" any activated mind state M, and with "o" any quiescent mind state M. The results are the expressions:

$$M^+ \text{ (activated mind)}$$
$$M^o \text{ (quiescent mind)}$$

Therefore M^o is a mind that does not seem responding to inputs, for example a person having an irreversible coma with cerebral death. On the other hand, M^+ is any mind which clearly shows specific answers to incoming stimuli or inputs. However, in some cases, even M^o could give some signs of life (some jerky muscular reactions of foot toes or Babinsky sign, of a patient in coma) but this does not indicate an attitude of that person to consciously react to inputs.

This is an important point, because, *in social, biological, and psychological sciences, minds are said to react to inputs only when an external observer could establish that that mind is reacting in "clear consciousness" to stimuli as the result of a "decision" to react given the opportunity also not to react.*

Neurological and automatic muscular reflexes in a person in a deep level of coma are not the result of his decision to react or not to react. Therefore, his mind is said to be quiescent.

These assumptions suggest us that we can place mind activities along a continuum going from a full state of alertness (resembling morbid excitement) to a state of quiet or coma. From our daily experience, we note that there is not a neat distinction between a fully activated mind, and a completely quiescent one. However, this distinction is not always clear, and only after many trials we feel confident that our mind is functioning in clear consciousness.

Other times, even when alert, a mind does not "want" to respond to stimuli, for example there is a focalized attention on a single event. Some states of hypnosis or advanced states of relaxation may illustrate this example. There is a clear consciousness but with mind seeming unresponsive to events. We can select to focus our attention to few, one, or even no events from our world. Responsiveness and unresponsiveness to stimuli are independent from mind activation. Therefore, we have alert and responsive minds, and alert and unresponsive minds. However, we can find non alert minds that show some degree of responsiveness. When brain is sick, it cannot be alerted but can respond to some elementary stimulation. After a head trauma, elementary responses can be evoked by the expert neurologist. The same applies in cases of a severe psychological trauma with apathy and mutism, for example in victims of a rape. Mind seems turned off but that person still can respond to some elementary stimulations: words, sympathetic approach, strokes, etc. The last example is found in a brain during cerebral death: there is neither alertness nor response to stimuli.

To summarize, states of alertness (responsiveness and unresponsiveness) are attitudes of mind, ways of choosing how to respond to stimuli. On the other hand, activation or quiescence is a way of reacting to stimuli, and is what is seen by an external observer.

A very brilliant and sympathetic person who is having is nap cannot be said to be an "unresponsive person", he is simply "quiescent". In fact, he is sleeping! The impression could be that when we ask him something he reacts as if he were deaf to our need. However, this is a false impression. He is simply tired and needs some rest!

2.5. Jumping to conclusions and the paradox of Zeus

One way to have faulty ideas is to jump to conclusions. Sometimes, our mind is an Olympic champion in jumps. Whenever possible, on the basis of some weak information, it arrives to solid and acritical conclusions. Greek philosophy was full of these examples, and a Greek shepherd of ancient time could have thought: "Zeus is a man, I am a man, and therefore I am Zeus". It seems a weak conclusion, but in some morbid pathologies, like in elated states of consciousness, hypomania, or even rage, these links are frequently found. A symbol that expresses the operation "if-then" is *modus ponens* (a Latin word) "⊃" and the symbol for therefore "∴". So, if we go back to the ancient Greek shepherd in a sort of mystic transportation, he is forming this thought process:

Considering the basic assumption that Zeus is like a man:

If M then Z (If I am a Man then I am like Zeus)	M ⊃ Z
M (I am a man)	M
Therefore Z (Therefore I am like Zeus)	∴ Z

Sometimes under strong emotions and elation, jumping to conclusions like this one is usual and familiar. How many parents have told to their children: "All parents should rule their children. We are your parents, *therefore* we rule you"? Or in a movie: "All pretty women will marry a millionaire. I am pretty, *therefore* I will marry a millionaire", that is translated in the expression:

"If I am pretty (P) *then* I will marry a millionaire (M). I am pretty (P). Therefore, I will marry a millionaire (M)"

$$If\ P\ then\ M$$
$$P$$
$$Therefore\ M$$

$$P \supset M$$
$$P$$
$$\therefore M$$

Loose connections between thoughts can be a problem in counseling setting. People are often upset ad stressed because of some conclusions they arrived having scarce information about how things are interrelated. Emotional breakdown, depression, elation, or strong affective crises all produce loose connections amongst concepts and ideas of the kind if-then. How many jealous partners say to their boyfriends: "If you are looking that woman then you don't love me anymore"?

However, paradoxes represent a fallacy in daily logics. Some people, during infancy, have received a total and unquestioned acceptance of their thinking because their families had no time or courage to rule them. These people are at risk of developing a narcissistic personality when adults. Logic fallacies derive from assuming that two opposite things can be equally true, as in the example: "This house is nice but I don't like it!". The question is: how can this person like something and dislike it at the same time? How can the house be nice and ugly at the same time? Is s/he saying the truth? Many times narcissistic thought is full of these logical paradoxes, because an unquestioned acceptance of what these people want and say leads them to live in relations where other people, for opportunity, do not question their fallacies. Apparently obstinate, they might feel hurt by someone who dares to question their fallacies. Therefore, the narcissist lives in a world where paradoxes are natural and logical! This being a paradox of the paradox. Other paradoxical expressions can be:

1. "I know that you are a lovable person but I do not love you!".
2. "Things can be nice but I thing that they are not!".
3. "I never feel that your work is well done and I don't say anything to you because I want to see if you change it the way I like!".

All these paradoxes claim for a simple logic representation:

$$A = \text{non } A$$
$$A = \neg A$$

Here, something can be itself and its opposite at the same time. Paradoxes may have some sense in drawings, like in Escher, but they jeopardize social relations of people holding and promoting paradoxes. Usually a paradox is defined as a statement or belief which is contrary to what is commonly known by common sense and by shared understanding.[8]

There are many cases in which isolated cultures and people hold to proper realities and logics that seem foreign to what is called "common sense". Yet, actual culture has an ethical responsibility in defining what should be considered common sense, considering that different cultures and ethnic groups hold different common senses. Nevertheless, by staying in our homes we face paradoxes almost daily, and depending on our susceptibility, we agree or not with paradoxical statements from other people. Truth is a matter of the average in paradoxical statements and not something which is shared as objective and singular. As in Escher drawings paradoxical realities seem having an autonomous life. We can survive close to people who hold different world views and perspectives, yet we can share the same fence and meet them at barbeques during weekends.

2.6. Final wonders in mind operations

Finally, if we like to impress our friends, what are the mental operations we can activate in order to show that our mind is going like a Ferrari car? We have seen at the beginning the game played by our mind in the Olympics. Really, they are logic operations (*and, or, if then, etc.*) and mental operations that allow us to treat, with some ease, complex stimuli from the world. We can add other categories that will somehow fill the tool box for having a mind well operating in the screening of incoming information. Following, some of these marvels we are able to perform with our mind.

First of all, we must distinguish that *something is part or not of something else.* If I tell to a woman that she is like any other, perhaps I am making a big mistake. If I cannot distinguish a poisonous rattle snake form a rope I am in a big trouble. What I need to do is to position things and information inside the right box or category. By mistaking a category I am at risk for a slap by a women or a bite from a rattle snake. The mental operation in this case uses the category symbolized by $x \in B$: *x is part of the set B.* Intending by "x" the single subject or object (my cat, my dog, my car) and with B the broader category that includes x (the whole class of cats, the whole class of dogs, the category of sport cars). If we take a fruit looking like an apple from a basket of apples, we feel confident in thinking that that juicy ball is "with some degree of certainty" an apple. But what happens if we take a number form an array seeming random? And what about in treating a cough as a symptom of flu instead of TBC? From the answers we understand how many people do daily research in order to give a sense to elements that seem casual or random. Let us take some number sequence (like some admission test at the college):

$$5, 32, 41, 113, 1112$$

What is the category? If x is any number of the sequence (with $x_1 = 5$, $x_2 = 32$, etc.) what is the category that might link them? Is there any relation amongst them? I think that most of you have already found the category! In fact the sum of the digit (d) in each number is always 5. Therefore "five" is the inclusive category for the numbers and the expression can become: *the sum of the digit of each number always gives five, or:* $\Sigma dx \in 5$. On the other hand, if something is foreign to a certain category we use the expression: $x \notin B$: *x does not belong to the set B.* For example, x is a neuron of the parietal cerebral cortex, while B is the set of neurons of the frontal area of the brain.

Another problem that our mind has to solve is *deciding if something exists or not.* During this last period many people were puzzled to establish if the Da Vinci Code exists or not. Often, my dilemma is simpler, and I want to establish what is the right ingredient to make an exceptional rice pudding. Other times researchers are looking for a curative therapy for a disease, or the anthropologist is seeking the missed tribe in the forest. No matter what the search is for, these scientists are using the category $\exists$, *exists.* Mind using this logic connective has mainly two other options:

1. $\exists x$, *there is at least one x, essential quantification.* For example, if I state that there is *at least one neuron n* implied for each thought process, I say: $\exists n$.

2. $\exists'x$, *there is only one x.* For example, if *n* is the number of attempts that a laser ray beam has to strike a target that is only one, we state that for striking the target the number of attempts a laser ray beam has, is just $\exists'n$.

Another puzzling decision our mind takes any time, is *predicting consequences.* In other words, it decides *if something is followed by something else.* Human physiology and pathology is based on this basic decision: Is a cerebral stroke always followed by a permanent loss of a neurological function? Is my action usually followed by your reaction? By indicating that something is not followed by something else I use the sign $\perp$, which means: *it is not linked or followed by.* We find this sign to indicate that a sequential process is not intervening, especially in sets. If I say that: "All *a* are *b*, but no *c is d*", I put the sign $\perp$ between c and d. If an increase in blood oxygen (bO_2) is not followed by an increased happiness ($\uparrow H$), I can decide to go to the ocean for the next summer instead of sharing my pancake with sweet-tooth bears of a mountain park:

$$bO_2 \perp \uparrow H$$

Strategic thinking usually developed in Economy for predicting the outcome in investments, broadly uses this category. Here, again, the importance of predicting consequences in the course of our daily decisions. We spend all our life in making connections and learning, but, mostly in discovering how natural phenomena, social actions, human relations are interrelated.

Finally, since we were children, we learned to predict how hard were our parents' punishments according to our tempra tantrums. Thinking about *how something is proportional to something else* makes life exciting because it helps us to experiment life dynamically. We will use the expression $\propto$: *proportional to.* For example, if *nc* is the number of cerebral neurones of the occipital cortex activated by the exposition of the retina to 1 lumen of light *l*, the number n of activated neurones is proportional to the number of lumen of lights: $nc \propto nl$. More simply, if cholesterol level is reduced by high intake of Omega fish factors, then there is a relation of proportion between the two data.

3   Working with our mind

3.1. How to familiarize with codes of our mind

This book is mainly concerned with the use of mathematical and logical expressions in order to illustrate the processes involved in thinking. Mathematical expressions have been used to shrink into few and simple concepts, different constraints of knowledge. In a sense, I have tried to use some simple mathematical or logical/symbolic expressions, in order to make understandable complex mind processes. What often happens in general mind theories is that the same concepts are explained with different theoretical frameworks, according to scientists' background. In this book, I tried to be synthetic but also aware of the possibility of using new ways of treating mind concepts by borrowing from living sciences some of their tools to explain difficult concepts. Simple algebraic and logic expressions seemed to me responding to this need. For this reason, I have tried to read mind processes in an alternative way, with some concepts borrowed from other science fields. In order to make things clear in this part, I would like to summarize some of these expression that nothing add to what is already known from college algebra, philosophy, logics, set theory, etc. I would like to think that if mind has invented all those symbols, then, in some sense, they represent a mirror of its own operations. In other words, these operations represent ways in which we master simple or complex tasks when we think.

3.2. Mathematical codes and mental operations

Mathematical codes perhaps represent the simplest mental operations we use in thought processes. No matter how many information we are trying to master or to organize, we always use some of these simplifiers in order to make our life simpler. One of the simplest decisions our mind makes is choosing if two or more things are similar. Are two cars of different colours somehow similar? If colour is an important discriminator they are not. Yellow is not the same as red. However, if we are not interested in colours, but in quality, two cars of the same company are really the same.

The basic operation we are using in this decision is: "$x = y$?". These are called variables, and our mind is performing a *similitude*. We are trying to decide if x and y are similar in some way, that is, if x *is the same as* y. These two variables can be two objects, two things, two pieces of information, or two people. Other times there are more than two variables, let us say 3. Things appear the same: "$x = y = z$?". This decision can be vital for some aspect of our life. If we decide that a rope *is the same as* a poisonous snake, we could have some trouble. Nevertheless, by applying the process of similitude we scrutinize the world of objects and concepts by a synthetic though process. In other words, we spare our mind efforts by avoiding different problem-solving for similar events. For this reason, it does not matter what car I am driving, I always employ the same skills I already own. Synthesis is a time sparing process for our mind, and it relies on similitude thought processes.

Differentiation is quite a similar process. Here what we do is to make distinctions between two stimuli, objects, and concepts. In this case, our mind is asking: "*Is $x \neq y$: is x different from y?*". Making distinctions is an important steps in selective though processes. For example, some people when depressed tend to generalize and to see different events as if they were the same. For the very depressed person all things "are the same", that is, sad. Even in normal circumstances, if we are disappointed by our boss, and we plan to look for another job, we are afraid to find another boss similar to the one we dislike. Therefore, making differentiations is important, and helps us to look at the world always as if it were offering us fresh and new inputs and stimuli, which means differentiated variables.

Making "more-less" distinctions is what helps us to distinguish things on the basis of "more" or "less" judgments. If something is more, or less, than something else, then it is important to know. More-Less thought processes, help us to master object, events, people according to categories of amount. This time our mind is trying to answer to: "*Is $x < y$, or is $x > y$?*". The sign "$<$" lesser than, and "$>$" greater than require the task of mastering proportions or rates. Also in this case, our life heavily depends on finding the right answer to more-less distinctions. If we have a bank account that is not extraordinary, and keep spending with our credit card sums without considering the incidence on our account, we are probably thinking that we are opulent and richer than we really are. This is a mistaken more-less thought process. Some psychopathologies show altered patterns of more-less categories. For example, people with severe paranoid personality disorder, like to think that other people are more rejecting towards them than their close friends or partners. Borderline personalities feel aggressive because live their life as if threatening events were "more" than usual, and believe that they are "less" protected than anyone else.

Almost-but-not-exactly-the-same operation is a way we use to master some objects or events that do not belong to the same categories. For example, number of losses and number of depressive episodes. Our mind is trying to answer to: "*Is x ≅ y? Is x almost the same than y?*". Things do not need to be similar. This would make the world flat. Much of our environment is shaped by things that are almost but not exactly the same. This opens the way to a healthy doubt which, in mind processes, is an open door to verify our assumptions and to change mistaken thought processes. Some obsessive-compulsive people do not feel satisfied until things are done exactly the way they have in mind. If two actions are not the same they are dismissed because unsatisfactory. If they do not cut their loan with straight lines as they did the week before, they feel miserable. The obsessive-compulsive is not accepting that things can be different, or that it is all right that two things are almost the same without being exactly the same. This is also called: "Accept the grey zones in your life!".

3.3. The renaissance man

With our minds we are able to perform almost the same operations that the Renaissance man performed. According to the degree of complexity we are familiar with, we use some basic operations that allow us to manipulate complex concepts and information. Although these operations belong to complex thought processes, we use them also for simple daily tasks. One question our mind is always tying to answer is if something belongs to a broader category. Deciding that flowers belong to plants, and that an eagle belongs to birds, are simple *categorizations*. We decided that the element alpha, eagle, is a member or not of a broader category A of all birds. We normally express this by symbols: "$\alpha \in A$: *Does the element alpha α belong ($\in$) to the set or category A?*". Categorization allows simplification and understanding. If I am able to predict that something belongs to a broader category I can understand this subset when I know the broader category. If I understand that something that has two wings that flies and deposits eggs in a nest is a bird, then I can predict other characteristics even thought that is the first time I meet that living creature. With the same mental process I can decide that something does not belong to a given category or that alpha does not belong to the set A: $\alpha \notin A$. The operation of categorization has practical applications in clinical psychology and psychotherapy. We have already met the process of categorization. We put in the same basket all apples that look alike. But we can put in the same basket apples with pears or peaches. Or considering that because your boss was unfair with you, any other boss (alpha) belongs to a category of people, bosses (A) that treat unjustly their employees. In some cases, when we are under pressure and depressed, we can think this way. There seems to be no signal that on Earth we can find a sympathetic and loving boss. In morbid cases, like in persecutory ideas, what is prevailing is a category A that will colour any other element of life, alpha. If a person has experienced abuse or neglect during childhood, s/he will categorize almost everybody as abusing and neglecting. If a woman has been victim of an abusing partner, she will consider any other partner as rude. And in face of the contrary, even a mild and sweet man is put inside the category "rude" because he is considered not sincere and masking his rudeness. We see that emotional and psychological factors have a primary role in directing our mind in choosing some of its own basic operations. Bias is always present although in different degrees of interventions. I would say that it is almost impossible to find unbiased ideas.

The symbol for Olympic Games is represented by five circles staying nicely together. In mathematics, sometimes circles are used to illustrate Venn Diagrams. Many concepts can be expressed as staying inside circles. They have a limit or boundary, and whatever is inside the circle is meant to share similar characteristics. For example, my family circle is made by my parents and sisters while your family circle is made by your spouse and your children. My circle and your circle have different qualities. They are also called sets. My family set is represented by my father "f", mother "m" and 2 sisters "s" and "s". Symbolically in set theory they are called members or elements of the set indicated by: m; f; s; s. My family set, on the whole is indicated by the capital letter F. Therefore: $F = \{m; f; s; s\}$. If your family circle F' is composed by your spouse "sp" plus a child "c" I know that: $F' = \{sp; c\}$. In this case, there are no similar members for the two circles. In other words, the two family sets do not overlap. But let us suppose that in your family circle there is your mother "m" still living with you, and because we are brothers, she is the same loving mother "m" of my family circle. We would then obtain that $F' = \{sp; c; m\}$. In this case "m" is found as shared between our family systems. Our family circles would become: $F = \{m; f; s; s\}$, $F' = \{sp; c; s; m\}$. A grandmother is an important person that we all like to have in our homes!

Belonging-to. If we use thought processes, our mind is always trying to see where to place some inputs or information, in what circle or set a bit of information belongs. In addition, if we have an external observer examining our families and he sees that we both have a grandmother in our families, his mind when examining my or your family, is trying to answer to: *Is $g \in F$: Is the grandmother an element that belongs to the set family F (or F')?* As with any other thought process, this operation would mainly allow *categorization*. This is a basic process that helps our mind to select and spare time and energy in examining inputs and information. When I go to the supermarket to buy vegetables, I put inside my trolley "T", a set, potatoes "p", beans "b", carrots "c", etc., these being members of a set.

I can summarize my exciting visit to the supermarket by writing home on a SMS: $T = \{p; b; c\}$. These are full of vitamins and healthy for our mind! However, as we can gain synthesis by using categorization, and by putting things inside the same basket, the same processes can hinder fine discrimination. There are people who like to generalize: they put different things inside the same basket. They try to over simplify things to the detriment of differentiation. Being able to distinguish what goes inside the same trolley helps us not to mix apples with meat. But when we pay scarce attention or we are tired or under the pressure of time, by using too much this process we move to some salad that is not exactly what we had in mind.

Not-belonging-to. How many times we felt sorry because our boss told us: "You do not belong to this company! You can keep for yourself your innovative and fancy ideas!". I hope not many times. Many new immigrants suffer from a depressive syndrome during their first period of stay in the hosting country: they feel they *do not belong to that culture*. If in my family F, I have a dog "d" that your family has not, then "d" does not belong to your family circle F'. Our mind says: *d does not belong to F': $d \notin F'$*. When I treat this category of thought process, it comes naturally to my mind to think about the example of immigrants. There are many people who can arrive to the conclusion that they do not belong to something important: a family, a club, a circle of friends. In their mind the category *"not belonging"* is present and activated by gestures of rejection by part of significant others. Violated children have a prevalence of "not belonging thought processes", as their mind is constantly concentrated on the feeling of rejection they experience in their own families or society. The task of attentive care takers will thus be that of reducing this category of prevailing thoughts by reinforcing perceptions of membership and affection.

Being-a-subset-of. Staying with mind processes informing us that something belongs to a wider category, we find another process of categorizing: for example having to decide if two categories are alike, one inside the other, one different from the other. In one instance, we have to decide if a category A belongs to another category B, and is totally inside it. The question is: $A \subset B$: *is A a subset of B?* For example, the group of college cheer leaders is a subset of all female students taking sport classes. With the symbol "$\subset$" we are saying that A is inside B or almost includes all the elements of B. For instance, apples are inside the category of fruit, and Mary, Susan and Donna are women and stay all inside the category "women". The same way, we can state that the category "women" (B) is a superset of the set Mary, Susan and Donna (A): $B \supset A$: *B is a superset of A.* The knowledge about subsets or supersets will facilitate our life. Other times, some elements are members or subsets of many other categories: for example Mary, Susan and Donna are members (subset) of the category "Tennis Club of Wonder City". Our ID cards often specify what our superset is: Library, Tennis Court, VISA holders, Frequent Flyers, etc. But the symbol "⊂" in psychology indicates that someone feels as being a member or not of a group, clan or family. We faced this aspect already before. "Being a subset", a mental operation, defines if we "feel we belong" (a psychological feeling), to something else. Many problems in life arise when we are missing this feeling of membership. In some sense, we feel foreign to some group where we would like to affiliate: family, friends, decisional board in the company, church party organizers, etc. The symbol "⊄" indicates this feeling of alienation by stating that a category A does not belong (or is a subset) (⊄) of another category B. In counselling theory, one of the efforts is to cancel in some clients the idea of "alienation". Because of some event, people suffer when feeling alienated, that is, when perceiving that they are out of some group (category) where they would like to belong. The need felt by many poor people of being someone, of being important, of having some values and importance in society are all expressions of this need. Their emotional attention is overestimating ⊄. And the result is that they are always focusing on activities or means that would cancel their inner feeling of separation.

To summarize, we have seen some mental processes that help us to put some elements, objects, information inside or not another broader category. Although these operations are universal and daily used in our lives, they can assume a preponderant weight in determining our feeling of alienation. Sometimes, we are not able to identify elements of a set, and we can say that it is an empty set or Φ. For example, thought contents of brain during a cerebral coma. The operations with categories are:

- $A \cup B$: *A united to B*. Set obtained by summing the sets of *A* and the sets of *B*. For example all students of Psychology class with all students with Psychotherapy classes.

- $A \cap B$: *A intersected to B*, elements that are in common between *A* and *B*. For example those students that are *enrolled* both in Psychology classes and Psychotherapy classes.

3.4. "To be or not to be" this is the problem

How many times are we involved in mental operations where the central task is to decide if something stays or not with something else? The two symbols from formal logics for expressing this puzzle are:

- $p \land q$: *p and q:* this is a conjunction, for example number of young people performing body piercing and number of young people having total body tattoos.

- $p \lor q$: *p or q:* this is a disjunction; for example, if *p* is the number and types of neurones in the occipital area activated during the exposition to a figure of a square, this cannot be *q* that is the types and number of neurones activated during the exhibition of a circle.

As an example of daily decisions, we will use the symbols "or/and" to decide where to go for a holiday trip. "Do I go to Florence or to Paris?", "Have I enough money for choosing mountains and lakes for my next journey?". *Decisional processes using "$\lor$" for "or" and "$\land$" for "and", belong to mental activities that help us to survive to multiple tasks or to information overload.* Making a choice between two alternatives is already demanding. Do I go to the beach (b) or to the lakes (l) for holidays? Which is symbolized by: "$b \lor l$?". However, if alternatives or information are more than two, let us say, beach (b), mountains (m), lakes (l), Europe (e) we can find multiple and alternating processes of and/or: $b \lor m \land l \lor e$.

There are some personality traits, like obsessive thinking, were these decisions are not simple. An obsessive person can ruminate for hours before deciding, if ever, where to go for holidays. Even strategic economic decisions may require some degree of these obsessive alternatives, by using "predictive scenarios". With this last I mean that before making a final decision, any person thinking rationally, like most of us, tries to imagine what would happen if one decision instead of another is taken. Predicting scenarios helps us to foresee the consequences of our decisions before these last are made. "What would happen if I choose "lakes" instead of "ocean"?". In symbolic logic there are not signs for codifying mind predictions! Almost all signs are intended for real decisions: and/or. But when I try a mental scenario of possible consequences of deciding something instead of something else, positive math, which has been created by positive people and not by psychologists, does not offer a lot. Therefore my quest is to find a symbol that I can use all the times I want, in order to indicate those precious instants that are spent to predict ("What if ...?") specific results of that particular mind operation. I thought I can use also in this case a symbol to specify this mind operation: what if? Let us say to use "ψ:" to recall the sign "Psi" used to denominate Psychology and followed by a colon to address the mind operation that follows it. Finally, if I am trying to predict (*what if)* what would happen if I choose mountains *m* and/or lakes *l* for holidays, I can synthesize this mental puzzle by:

$$\psi : m \vee l$$

$$\psi : m \wedge l$$

What-if mind operations denote a profound and mature understanding of our world and our actions. Unfortunately, there also people who are weak in predicting core consequences to their own actions following certain mental operations. This weakness in *what-if* operations, create conditions for forming weak predictions. As a child, these people are unwilling or unable to predict future and probable scenarios of their decisions, and would act impulsively when making important choices. In some morbid cases, like in hypomania and mania (also from a chemical intoxication, alcohol abuse, etc.), *what if* operations are missing and a person is completely driven by immediate impulses and choices. This is sometimes seen also in antisocial people where impulses have a prevailing part over problem solving.

3.5. Predicting the future

Predicting consequences of actions or facts is one of the mental operations that help us to survive. Having many data in our hands is not so important as being able to use them to see what would happen if they are used or arranged in a different way. All predictions usually follow "if-then" logics in order to assess consequences and to predict future events. As we have seen previously also prediction of the if-then category need an initial mental operation: Psi factor ψ or "what-if" that reminds us that all our predictions about future are influenced by our psychological state at the moment of prediction. In other words, pessimism and optimism influence the probabilistic scenario that we have in our minds when we predict future events of the kind if-then. Having said that, the logic expression for if-then is "$\Rightarrow$" and the cases are:

$$\psi: r \Rightarrow g$$

If I know that *if* it rains (*r*) *then* plants will grow (*g*), in that case a good prediction is forecasting what I can do if anytime it rains plants grow. For example, having this if-then information I can decide to choose a land in a humid and rainy part of the country, if I want to harvest plants which need a lot of water. I can make good business by having two basic information: a) an "if-then" piece of information (if it rains then plants grow), and ii) a "what-if" applied to "if then", where I start to think about a future set of actions according the information that rain helps some plants grow. To summarize if-then operations, we have:

1. $r \Rightarrow g$: *r implies g, if r then g*: if it rains plants grow.
2. $r \Leftarrow g$: in this case I make a scientific prediction by saying that also the opposite is true: if plants grow than it rains. Perhaps, by having a big forest, then air humidity increases and this would facilitate raining. In fact, desertification is a consequence of the reduction of plants.
3. $\therefore$, *therefore, as a consequence.* For example, if high blood sugar (BS) rises the level of insulin secretion (IS), and if a long term high level of insulin secretion is responsible for diabetes (D), the cascade of consequence is: BS $\Rightarrow$ IS; IS $\Rightarrow$ D; therefore: $\therefore$ BS $\Rightarrow$ D, that means that *as a consequence* a high level of blood sugar could be held responsible for diabetes.

In psychology, but also in a normal unbiased thinking, both effects should be deemed to be true, $r \Rightarrow g$ and $r \Leftarrow g$. This concept of evaluating data from a bilateral deterministic perspective is basic in psychotherapy, and in abandoning altered cognitive schemes. For example, many morbid thought disorders are deterministic because a person assumes an erroneous consequential direction of unrelated events. A depressed person many times uses consequential thinking with the application of the implication "$\Rightarrow$": "If my husband is moody (*m*), then I feel depressed (*d*)". She is assuming as true $m \Rightarrow d$, which means that she feels that her depression is determined by how the husband reacts. However, in psychology, there are no unilateral explanations, and people "cannot make other people feel the way they feel": it is a personal choice feeling depressed, instead of excited, annoyed, and neutral. Therefore, in family therapy there can be another way of reading facts. That is, that moodiness of the husband is a consequence of wife's depression. This would also admit the expression: *if d then m,* $d \Rightarrow m$.

A singular and exciting way of considering guesses, are self-fulfilling predictions. In other words, some events seem occurring just because someone has predicted them. First recognized in politics and in polling (candidates being or not elected because resulted favoured in prediction), they have also a tremendous impact in psychology. It can happen that some unwanted behavior in a person can occur just because someone has predicted him and exposed him this prediction. This is frequent with children: "If you keep jumping you will fall!". What will happen to that child? S/he will fall! According to Merton, the first to mention this term, a "self-fulfilling prophecy is a "false" definition of the situation evoking a new behavior which makes the originally false conception come "true".[9] There are many people, with a passive-aggressive personality, who, in order to contradict other people's statements, act in a way to make those statements true. Youngsters drink alcohol if they have an authoritarian father always telling them: "You should not drink alcohol. It's bad for your health!". Or even more, "If you continue to drink you will get liver cirrhosis". People to whom these statements are addressed, enter in a circle of contradictions, and start to drink just when hearing these warnings. There are many fields where self-fulfilling prophecies have been studies. They have positive effects in education, where teachers expecting that a student will be "smart" will behave in a way to elicit smartness of that student. This is called "self-fulfilling aspect of teacher expectancy", while "trend project as self-fulfilling in economy" means that predicting an economic development will "cause" certain social adjustment to make this prediction true.[10]

3.6. Fine discrimination

Our daily experiences are not based exclusively on differences or on things that happen or not. There are sectors in our life where mental processes help us to establish when something is increasing. The sign delta Δ is used to define an increment. A real discrimination of differences and the perception that some and important change has occurred, is a matter of understanding shades of information and to avoid oversimplification. If we know that when it is raining too much, that can be dangerous for a flood, we can activate our coping strategies to see if we can do something to avoid that water fills our cellar. Discriminations can be applied to any dimension and measure. More-less discriminations applied to the physical world relates to time, weight, length, etc. Other more-less psychological discriminations are also possible and less obvious. For example, we discriminate if we feel more or less anxious, more or less depressed, more or less tired. These evaluations also help us to activate coping strategies for lowering the risk of nervous breakdown. In any instances, in discrimination we should have some basic understanding that something has changes from a state x to a state x_1. This is something magic because our mind somehow arbitrarily assigns a value to any unit it is evaluating, physical or psychical, and then establishes that a mutation of this unit is in a degree which is significant to be considered valuable. In fact, our mind is not alerted, let us say, for any change between x (i.e., raining) and x_1 (i.e., raining more than expected). However, anyone is able to say that in a rainy day it is raining "more" than any other day of the week. Yet, no one uses graduated bottles in the garden to say that in the bottle there is more water than other days. We simply say that today is "more" than yesterday. And most of the times we are right. Our mind has embedded computational processes in order to establish that something is more or is less than something else without using meters or other devices. The sign used to indicate variations is delta Δ. Therefore a variation in time t is indicated by Δt, while a variation in the amount of daily rain r can be specified by Δr. But as we can use a rod to measure a street, how do we measure an increase or decrease in depression, anxiety, boredom? If we are able to do it, then it means that our mind has embedded mechanisms of self-detection (because psychological states are internal to the same mind) in order to assess levels of emotional states. In addition, there would be an arbitrary way our mind uses in order to define the "unit" that measures depression, anxiety, etc. Therefore, something changes from depression x to depression x_1, or from anxiety x to anxiety x_1. Fine discrimination is often a matter of experience. As anyone knows, an Esquimo is able to discriminate up to 100 types of snow flakes. An experienced sommelier can discriminate amongst different wines. Perhaps learning helps us to make fine discriminations. Finally, many scientists are able to make important discoveries because capable to make fine discriminations. Yet what is the unit of depression or anxiety that makes us say that something has changed? Do we detect internal cortisol or adrenal levels in order to say that we are more depressed and anxious?

3.7. Let us familiarize with our brain

Science has made giant steps in neurosciences and cognitive theories to clarify the ways our brain works. We know a lot on how our brain functions, and on how it looks like in its areas. I would say that there is a tremendous amount of data, scientifically confirmed about brain functions, cognitive processes, neuropathology, neuroimaging, etc. Each day, secrets in functions of our brain become of public domain, and people understand basic psychology and psychopathologies, the effects of brain injuries, new therapies for brain abnormalities, etc. We are personally aware of what could make our thinking easier: i.e. being in a comfortable room, feeling relaxed, having a good self-esteem, having a loving family, and a rewarding job. But when we slightly move from these optimal situations, something seems changing. A woman has injured her finger while cooking for a dinner. She was worried because her husband met a bad storm while on his way to home, and was not giving news about him at the cell phone. Anxiety and fear of that woman were impeding clear thinking, and she was not able to go on with her cooking. The life of her husband was her major concern. Even in simple occasions, when air conditioning is broken in the library, some college students find it difficult to study in a hot summer. Their mental process, and we are sure about this!, are all right, but a slight increment in air temperature and humidity is such to make clear thinking an important effort. Memory seems impaired. The whole body is concentrated on heat sensation, thirst, and the mental image of being at the shore. If we want to make our first drawing of thinking and the influence of external factors on it, we can imagine something like the Figure 3.7.1. With the word "Environment" we can interpret any physical factor that surrounds us and hinders clear thinking: noise, air temperature, humidity, food, alcohol, etc. From the Venn diagram we infer that emotions too are affected by "environment". That is, why we feel nervous and anxious in a crowded room, with a high percentage of carbon monoxide, high humidity, and high temperature. In these conditions, also an expert astronaut would make extra efforts to think clearly (see Apollo 13 movie). Moreover, when clear thinking becomes difficult, *errors* appear. Errors, as mentioned in this book, are common in our life. Biases or omissions are forms of errors. It is not the evil part of our thinking, but if errors are frequent, and appear in most of our coping strategies, we must think that the process of thinking is under the influence of strong emotional or environmental factors, and that our life itself is at risk. Something is forgetting a toast in the toaster. Something else is forgetting a basic procedure in an operation of heart surgery or in the check at the panel of an aircraft. But errors are unavoidable. In order to prevent *errors in thinking* we must have clear what processes are at the moment influencing the freshness of our ideas: Are emotions? Anxiety? Anger? Heat? Humidity? Food intoxication with bowel turmoil? Finally, we can see that also emotions influence thinking, and they can facilitate (for example, a state of happiness), or hinder (for example, sadness) clear thinking.

Figure 3.7.1.—The Reciprocal influence of emotions and environment upon mental processes

EMOTIONS ⇒ THINKING ⇐ ENVIRONMENT

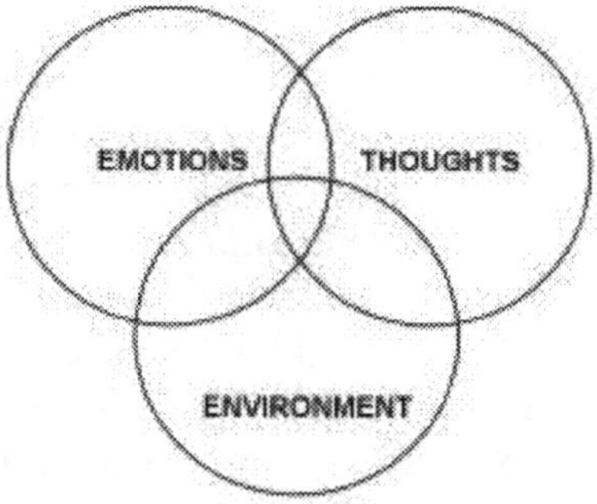

Let us try to express these events by using an algebraic expression:

$$\text{Thinking (T)} = 1/(\text{Emotions (E)} \times \text{Environment (En)})$$

This is to say that the whole process of thinking is inversely proportional to the effects of Emotions and Environment. By condensing the formula we get:

$$T = 1/(E \times En)$$

Here, thinking T (let's say clearness in problem-solving) is somehow inversely proportional to Emotions and Environment. These two last can have additive effects on T. In other words, if E and En increase their value (or influence) T becomes smaller. Can we think clearly in a state of full rage because our partner has just left us and we are in broken car under the rain in an isolated road? *Errors* are big when clear thinking is weakened. But errors in thinking, as we have just seen, are determined by the increase in our emotional turmoil and hindrances from environment. All theses causes (and even more) somehow negatively influence thinking and make *errors* more frequent. If we call errors with the Greek letter ε, and thinking with the Greek letter τ, we feel excited in finding that:

$$\varepsilon = 1/\tau = E \times En$$

Or, just changing the order of the factors:

$$\varepsilon = E \times En = 1/\tau$$

So, now we understand why we made a mistake in our budget report to our boss, that special day when our wife called us because se lost her Credit Card while she was at the most expensive boutique in the town, while our son broke our car by trying to use it for a cross country raid! We might show to our boss that our mistake was not our fault but depending by the (ExEn) factor. Let us hope that our boss is a person who likes math! But what part has our brain with τ, ε, E and En? If our brain is a box (thanks God that it is not so simple!), we find inside it τ (thinking), ε (errors) like a result of τ, E (emotions), and the effect of environment En (also a high blood pressure represents the Environment that our brain deals with, like cholesterol, glycaemia, anoxia, etc.). Let us go back to our brain as a box. Actually the basic units of our brain are neurons. If we are familiar with brain morphology shown by some TV programs, we remember that neurons form a sort of *network* or net where they communicate with each other by axons and dendrites. They are living entities. And our process of thinking is also a living and dynamic process. Therefore, in order to emphasize the flow of thinking, I would like to use the Greek letter delta Δ which somehow identifies processes of variation: mainly increase or decrease.

$$\tau = \Delta\tau$$

Fig. 3.8.2.—A functional representation of neurones and axons as they can be imagined in a reciprocal array for co-operation.

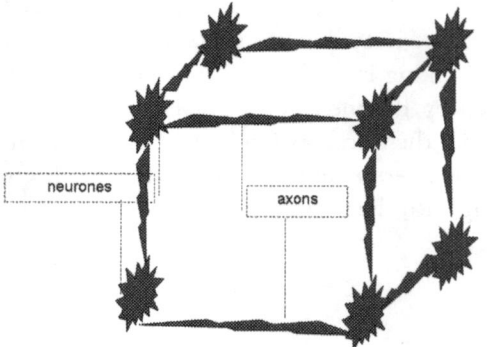

If our wife has decided to go to the best boutique in the town, and she is looking for the best choice talking with her friends, she very much has a positive increase in Delta: there is much planning, evaluating, choices, etc. While if we have decided to stay home just watching on TV the last football game of our favourite team, seating on a cosy chair, we are not using τ very much, and Delta is shifting to assume negative values (we just think less and enjoy more!).

Let us go back to our brain that resembles a box, and to our neurons that resemble stars with their beams. In this case, in order to imagine the simplest functional unit that is involved in the birth of a thought, we might think about a box that has on his corners neurons linked or communicating to the adjacent ones. The small stars in the corners are neurons. I ask for some indulgence to neuroscientists for this simplification! However, I am trying, like an astronomer, to portray the initial moment when a thought is formed: the brain Big Bang. Let us say that some neurons, all at once, decided to start a game. One of them, the neuron with more initiative that we call Fred, tells to other neurons: "Let's start a game!". Other neurones ask him: "What game?", and he replies: "Let's think!". And this is the beginning of all! I am not familiar with neurons that play the role of pacemakers. Perhaps the Reticular Activating System, in the Brain Stem, has a function of alerting the whole cerebral cortex. Severe damages of this centre somehow placed in our neck, may lead to cerebral coma. Let stay with Fred. Fred, the activating neuron, is playing in a cerebral area, and is trying to find a math solution. Today he feels excited. Fred wants to help his master (actually the owner of the brain) to find a solution about the shortest route to go to the shore. There is some familiarity between Fred and the process of thinking. In other words, each neuron is functionally constructed in order to express its own activity via neuro-mediators and electrochemical impulses. No matter what he does, Fred is a good boy and when his master, Mr Creative, asks him to think, he does it very well. Neuron Fred, is the boss for thinking. Now, if we call Fred with N and his friends too with N, when they all play "thinking" in the box, the game is represented by 8 players (8 corners in the box) interacting in order to reach their goal: a basic unit of thinking.

$$8N = \Delta\tau$$

Good score! But the game could be played even by more neurons. For complex games like thinking how to drive a space shuttle, the master needs to alert the whole team of his cerebral neurons. How many? I do not know. Let us say an infinite number ∞ of Neurons:

$$\infty N = \Delta\tau$$

Wow! That is incredible. A game where players (N) are so intermingled and friendly to each other that the master is able to guide a space shuttle in the Universe!

Well! As long as Emotions (E) and Environment (En) are under control, Neurons can play a good game, and the master (each one of us while thinking) reaches the solution that is useful to solve intricate problems in space travels. So, if CO (Carbon Monoxide) increases in the cabin, and the master feels home sick after a month of space travelling, and his co-pilot has a bad flu, errors ε in thinking and judgments are highly probable.

To summarize: Emotions and Environment affect the physiology and function of Neurons, and finally alter thinking. This leads to a positive increase in errors. The following formula illustrates this process.

$$\Delta E + \Delta En \Rightarrow \infty N \Rightarrow \tau \Rightarrow \pm\Delta\varepsilon$$

All factors are variables, and the formula is dynamic in the sense that it changes any moment. As a consequence, the process of thinking is just the arithmetic mean (M) of the sum Σ of the former expression:

$$\{M\ [\Sigma(\Delta E + \Delta En \Rightarrow \infty N \Rightarrow \tau \Rightarrow \pm\Delta\varepsilon)]\}$$

4 The "games" our mind plays

4.1. The workaholic neurons

One simple hypothesis I would like to make about the game cerebral neurons play is that they are basically in an *activated or inactivated mood, that is, a neuron can be on an ON or OFF state of excitement.* Neuronal transmission mostly operates by a threshold model: if the excitement is below the threshold, the neuron does not send neurochemical impulses to adjacent neurons. If the threshold is affected, neuron Fred is able to talk with closer friends. A way to express the ON and OFF state of excitement of a neuron is by using a *binary code with the number 1 expressing the state of excitement, and 0 expressing the state of rest.* So, if our team of 8 neurons with Fred as captain is playing the game "Thinking", the activity of all 8 players depends on the difficulty of the game. If the game is simple, perhaps Fred will alert only two other players. For more complex games (and thinking), the whole team is alerted and working. For example in a simple game the pattern of the team is

11000100

For a more complex game:

11100111

Etcetera.

If the problem I have to solve is how to sharpen my pencil, the first pattern is sufficient. A more complex pattern with more neurons activated is needed if I have to pilot a space craft or to perform a neurosurgical operation. Now, as we have seen before, the two numbers that express a state of alert is one (1) and zero (0) for a state of quiet. Some neurons work better together. In any moment we find a certain amount of excited neurons in the state 1, and another amount of neurons in the quiet state 0. This variation in number is always indicated by Δ which, in this case, can signal the variation in *number* (and not in the state of excitement which responds to the law of all or nothing) of excited neurons:

$$\pm\Delta(1) + \pm\Delta(0)$$

Or, which is the same, summing up the number N of neurons in the state 1 and the number N of neurons in the state 0.

$$\Sigma N(1) + \Sigma N(0)$$

But neurons that are not working do not bother a lot. We can leave them while are taking a nap. What we like most are the Stakhanovist neurons, those working most of the time. Therefore the previous expression becomes:

$$\Sigma N(1)$$

and finally:

$$\tau = \Sigma N(1)$$

This expression, in our example, could fit the algebraic representation of a single operation of thought to the point that for any given though unit (see later for the meaning) we have a certain amount of neurons in a state 1, and another amount in the state 0. If I am in a boat, fishing on a quiet river, the number of my neurons in state 1 is quite low. I have chosen to have a tranquil holiday, no matter how, and I have turned off almost all my neurons! Another business is fishing on the Amazon River, with a small boat with the risk of crocodile assault. This time the whole team, Fred and other neurons are alerted to allow me to fish a big cat fish.

We are not saying that quiet neurons are not useful. They, as we will see, just with their laziness increase the qualities of neurons 1 to the point, that if all neurons were working in a given time T we would be in a sort of overexcitement. For example, this could happen in epilepsy where a disordered, generalized, and arrhythmic activity involves the whole brain. Taking some addiction drugs activates the cerebral cortex and other cerebral centers to the point that information is fussy and no clear idea can be formed. Let us say that for a physiological problem-solving we need only a *certain amount* of excited neurons. They make the pool B of the set A which represents the total amount of cerebral neurons. In this case B is a part or subset of the set A. This fact can be expressed with:

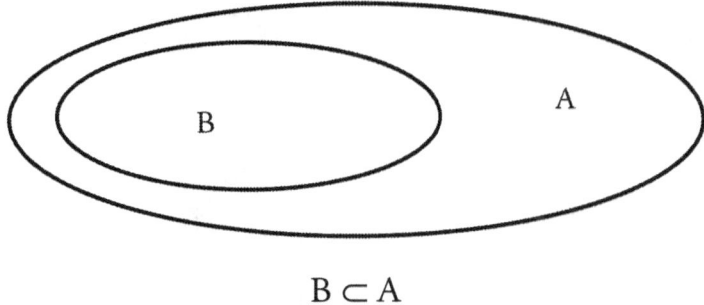

$$B \subset A$$

When B = A, for example in some circumstances of panic attack or strong fear like in conditions close to death, a person is somehow crystallized and unable to think because terrified, depersonalized, derealized, etc. In the state of stupor or even cerebral death B = 0, while in a state of generalized cortical activation $B \cong A$, ($\cong$ means "almost similar to"). Therefore, if we go back to our team with our friend Fred, playing a quiet game of problem-solving, we can find that the amount of active players (N_B) during the championship are somehow between the whole league players A and no player playing at all:

$$0 < N_B < A$$

(The first sign "0 <" means that N_B is greater than zero, while the second sign "< A" tells us that N_B is not representing the total number of neurons of the whole brain). By going back to previous expressions about excited neurons, we get a first algebraic expression about thoughts:

$$\text{if } N = \Sigma N(1)$$
$$\text{and}$$
$$\text{if } \Sigma N(1) = \tau$$

Then, *functionally speaking,*

$$0 < \tau < A$$

This means that any process of problem solving τ activates a number of neurons N which is between zero cerebral neurons activated and all cerebral neurons activated.

But A, the bulk of all our neurons, is given by the sum of all total activated and quiet neurons. And we have seen before this expression. Now we can substitute A with:

$$0 < \tau < [\Sigma N(1)]$$

This expression tells us that *any thought process implies the activation of a certain number of neurons ranging from something more than 0 (in case of cerebral coma) to a number which is the sum Σ of activated Neurons N(1).*

This is a neuro-functional expression at a given time T. Consequently, we deduce that in any moment, the smallest unit of thought τ is never 0! We need almost one playing neuron N to accomplish the simplest form of a thought: for example when we drive from work to home. But a single or complex idea can never equal the activity of the total number of functional neurons A, which, as we have seen, could lead to the paradox of high cerebral activation and confused ideas. A sort of electroshock. There are pathological thought process resulting from the inactivation of the brain or its over arousal. The expression for a thought disorder τ$_{dis}$ is then:

$$0 \cong \tau_{dis} \cong A$$

This is to say that we have a thought disorder when there are few or too many activate cerebral neurons. This is the basis for the birth of false thoughts, biases, and errors ε. So we arrive to the point to say that if I am under anesthesia for a surgical operation I cannot perform problem solving because my brain is somehow sleeping: τ ≅ 0. Whereas, if I had an experimental injection of caffeine (this is only an hypothesis!) above a physiological level my brain is inside a mess and also in this case I cannot think clearly: τ ≅ A. In both instances, the chance of having mistaken thoughts is high, even if I can dream under anesthesia for surgery, or if I can have artistic and creative hallucinations after the injection of caffeine (if possible). In these instances, τ ⇒ ε, which means that faulty thoughts and mistaken judgments are numerically high. The previous expression can be changed to the following:

$$0 \cong \varepsilon \cong A$$

This is the same:

$$\tau_{dis} \Rightarrow \varepsilon$$

From here, a general conclusion: *errors are the natural consequences of mental under-activation or over-activation. This is conductive to mistaken thoughts, biases, and vice versa.*

4.2. Again emotions and environment

If I am in front of a lion in the bush, or dating my girlfriend, or even drinking the most delicious beer in the world, Emotions (E) and Environment (En) prevail on clear thinking. How can I think clearly if my girlfriend has accepted to eat a pizza with me? Thinking in clear consciousness with a strong influence of E and En is not easy, and we are keen to accept as reliable the sweet words that a kind person is whispering to our ears. Emotions and Environment are somehow affecting (we do not say negatively) the process of thinking to the point that the risk for an increased error ε is high. I might decide to desert math lessons to be at the basket field when my girlfriend is playing with her team. In a moment of full love, even concentration and study become difficult. I do not eat. I start to have nightmares when she is not responding anymore to my attention. As we have seen before, also without becoming obsessive-compulsive people, some amount of clear thinking requires an acceptable control in the overload of emotions and environmental factors. Even artists, performers, and creative people need to apply bridles to their fantasy and emotions in order to channel their energy into a perfect performance. A pianist, who totally responds with emotions to a Chopin's concert, is close to make a poor performance (many errors in touch, expression, rhythm). Therefore, mistakes are directly influenced by disturbing Emotions and Environmental factors:

$$\varepsilon \Leftarrow E \wedge En$$

4.3. Time factor

Brain, for sure, is not plate. We can know someone with a flat mind, highly biased, but his brain is not flat! We live in a tridimensional world, and time is one of these dimensions. Time is a factor important for thinking. Something is to find a fast and reliable solution. Something else is to have time to find a solution for an important problem. Any final solution to a problem is a process that has involved thinking for a time. Therefore: *Solution = Time × Thinking*. Time can have any dimension: minutes, hours, years. Some problems are so difficult that we spend almost our life to find a solution. Some spiritual topics might belong to this category. However, what about thinking for finding an empty parking lot? Perhaps we need some minute to solve this issue. In some extent, thinking τ is similar to the expression that links it to the variation of time ΔT. Therefore we have:

$$\tau \equiv \Delta T\tau$$

Now, we try to think about the total amount of time T we have employed to solve a complicated problem: i.e. how to fix our laptop infected by a dangerous virus. In this case ΔT equals the sum Σ of all simple thought processes τ during sequential times t_1, t_2, t_3 etc. Therefore, if I want to tell to my girlfriend that I would appreciate her help during next weekend to paint the garden fence, at time t_1, I decide to take her out for a dinner, at time t_2, I give her a nice bush of flowers, at time t_3, I whisper her some nice words, and at time t_4, I ask her to help me. What I do during each fraction of time t is a fragment of thinking τ, of the whole process of problem-solving, that should lead me (if I am lucky enough) to have a positive answer by my girlfriend. At the end, I can surprise my girlfriend, if she paints the fence together with me, explaining her that my success was partly due to the following expression:

$$\tau = \Delta T\tau = \tau t_0 + \tau t_1 + \tau t_2 + \ldots \tau t_n$$

In addition, if I express my surprising and final result, a religious painting, with Ω which in theology expresses the Lord as being the Alpha and the Omega, we obtain:

$$\Omega\tau = \tau t_0 + \tau t_1 + \tau t_2 + \ldots \tau t_n$$

If we are believers, we spend part of our life in answering important questions about our existence in order to reach a pale understanding of the almighty goodness $\Omega\tau$. We should also not be surprised, that in some extent, as Victor Frankl said, we are sense seekers, and have an innate impulse for the search of meaning. There is always a beginning moment at t_0 when we decide that it is the moment to question ourselves about profound issues that can be spiritual, mathematical, ethical, physical, biochemical, and so on. I would treat the beginning of the process of thinking as a magic moment. It is when we seat and tell to ourselves: "Well Bob this it the right moment to think about …!". This is the magic beginning. The Lord was familiar whit man's natural quest for truth to the point to indicate Himself as the "Beginning" for this quest, but also the End. If we briefly think about the spirituality of thinking, and what we get with our mind, by ourselves, and the great amount of operations and probability problems we simply use to cross the street not to be invested by a car, we understand how important $\Omega\tau$ is. It is so important, that I would like to celebrate with you the beginning of everything, that is τt_0 with the expression α (the first thought). Therefore, the previous expression can now assume its symbolic representation of thinking in:

$$\Omega\tau = \alpha + \tau t_1 + \tau t_2 + \dots \tau t_n$$

What still surprises me a lot is that anyone is familiar with the decision that we make and that sounds in our mind as: "Let's think about!". We should imagine a sort of pacemaker, a sense seeker inside our mind, that any time, is telling us what mental operations are important to get a sense out of our magic world. As long as we are able to think, nicely mixing emotions, love, environment, fantasy, etc., our thinking will run smoothly. The process of human thinking, no matter how complex, can always proceed faster than any thinking machine. Even errors can be an alternative path to problem-solving, this process being called serendipity. Many important discoveries were made by an alternative perspective in looking at reality.

While, in a hypothetical thinking machine (i.e., our laptop), errors are simply the natural result of processes that proceed along one-dimensional and longitudinal pathways, human problem-solving can use alternative pathways by making, in few seconds, probabilistic calculations for the best alternative.

If a train stops no other train can pass. Humans can think about several options: passengers of that train might take a horse and ride towards tourist villages on the cost. I have never seen a creative machine! As we will see later, our brain is able to imagine infinite forms of logics, not simply based on longitudinal data processing like *if-then*. Many machines are *if-then* thinkers: my computer, that I still love so much, tells me: "If you push this then I show you that". Or something similar. If I am dating my girlfriend and I treat her with an *if-then* logic ("If I send her flowers than she will accept my invitation"), I am quite sure that she will be offended, and will burn my letters immediately.

If we go back to the previous math expression, we can say now that in a thinking machine, α is always external. They must be turned on by a person. Even if in some movies there are scenes about robots that turn themselves on and off, that think better than humans, that perform better than humans, the problem is to invent a *pacemaker* that tells to the machine: "Hi Fred: lets warm up your chips and think your manner". Perhaps future bio-machines, than can inherit from man his sense seeking inclination, could also mirror perfectly human thinking. Now, let us familiarize with robots, thinking machine, microchips, etc., to teach them how to start thinking and self-activate themselves. In other words, for exercise, we want to build an intelligent machine, with a self-activating device, in order to understand what mental processes are involved in delicate processes of problem-solving in humans.

4.4. Creating models

Let us think that we want to create HR, a sophisticated home robot that has all the power to substitute us in our daily and boring tasks. Well, we are familiar with the film Matrix but what I would like to focus on is how to create a sort of peacemaker microchip that would help a robot in ordinary thinking ("Hi HR! Warm up your own chips, and think your manner!"), and random thinking. Let us say that one day, autonomously, my home robot decides to paint my fence. Another other day HR decides to help my partner in cooking the turkey for the Independence Day. In order to tackle these tasks, we bought HR in a flee market or garage sale. We were sophisticated enough that we knew exactly what HR was able to do, that is, its own $\Omega\tau$. However, now, we have not all that time to teach to our home robot what its task is for the running day: cutting the loan, cleaning the porch, helping to take leaves out of the swimming pool. In other words, we know that *robots are not able to self-activate to randomly process data in order to decide autonomously what to do and in what order.* This is too difficult! Therefore, in order to reduce errors, we have already put a microchip into HR "mind" giving it the right sequence of performances: washing dishes, before cutting the loan, and painting the fence before washing the car. Somehow, we used *if-then* logics to program HR. But we are obstinate. If we are not home we would like that our home robot be able to wake up by itself, and start to follow the program "House Keeping". *Somehow, we have still to reach the solution on how to teach a model to become its own pacemaker in order to self-activate the starting process of thinking* α. Only by teaching robots how to self-activate, we obtain a model that resemble the way in which our processes of problem-solving begins.

This helps us also to reflect on ourselves, and to understand how and why we decide to think and how we find solutions to problems. If problem-solving depends on a physiological need, then we are not different form the cave man that was a clever hunter and perfection himself in order to bring more preys to his cave to feed his family. If we are like renaissance artists and sensitive in our souls, we are similar to a painter or a musician that likes to understand the world and its secrets by creating the best canvas or writing the best music of all centuries. If we reason like post-modern humans, we like to integrate objective science with spirituality, or to give a sense to topics that are not immediately similar. No matter what our basic needs are, alpha factor α (*the starter of problem-solving*) seems coming from an inner urge, that is, somehow linked to our spiritual and physical existence. If we indicated this need with ν, then we obtain that *alpha* depends or is started by ν:

$$\nu \Rightarrow \alpha$$

This expression simply means that *if we have a need (physical, psychological, social, etc.), we start to think about how to solve it.* But if we start to think, then, usually we arrive to the solution of this need or Ω (which means, the final solution). When the Lord says that he is the Alpha and the Omega, the beginning and the end, and that we will satisfy our quest for meaning only accepting Him, he has indicated the core of any human thinking:

Need $\rightarrow$ Beginning of thinking $\rightarrow$ Solution of the need

$$\nu \Rightarrow \alpha \Rightarrow \Omega$$

By making some substitutions, we finally obtain the *first dynamic expression of thinking*:

$$\Omega\tau = \nu + \tau t_1 + \tau t_2 + \dots \tau t_n$$

To go back to our home robot HR, and if we want to give it a human resemblance, we must create a sort of inner need in it that will be self-detected as a proper need. In some movies, scary robots self-turn them on when they somehow "perceive" a threat from outside. This need must be of such a dimension that by not solving it the robot will self-destruct. Similarly, if a person, who was not loved during childhood, denies his need for love and strokes when adult, he will probably develop severe personality disorders. Psychotherapy of this adult aims to teach him how to recognize his need for affection, and how to solve practical problems about how to collect positive strokes to feed his need for love.

Therefore, the perception of the need ν simply adds a factor π (Greek "p" for perception of the need). The first dynamic expression of problem-solving will assume the following form of the *second dynamic expression* of thinking:

$$\Omega\tau = \pi\nu + \tau t_1 + \tau t_2 + \dots \tau t_n$$

No matter what the thought process is, it cannot have a beginning without a perceived need. This last requires a whole sequence of actions of problem-solving in order to satisfy this need. We can assume that any unsolved need always increases cerebral activation as an alert mood that asks for the final solution of the need itself. In addition, we can also assume that our brain considers $\Omega\tau$ as final solution as long as it shows to be an acceptable and viable solution for the perceived and initial need $\pi\nu$.

If we apply these concepts to the construction of our "intelligent" home robot, able to self-activate according to the existence of a need, we can insert somewhere in its internal electronic circuits a sensing machine like that shown in the figures below. For those who are reading and considered a timer, I would like to congratulate with them for the idea, and add that even humans have internal clocks that regulate their biorhythm: i.e. hormone secretion, level of blood cortisol, etc. What we really are trying to do is to assign to our home robot some tasks of thinking process with a need-sensor, like we already have as humans, in order to understand how the thinking process starts. The core process needs a device able to detect the levels of a basic need in this robot, like a *sensor*, that, when alerted, starts the thinking processes in HR (let us say the initial switch ON). Only when this sensor is activated, our home robot will autonomously proceed to solve all problems for which it is regulated.

I have modified HR, that was bought in a flee market as a robot of the first generation, in order to set its basic needs according to the level of maple syrup (this never lacks in my home!) in a small internal tube. This tube has a level sensor at the top, where it is totally filled, that generates a state of model satisfaction $\Omega\tau$. Here, HR has accomplished all its problem-solving and is not activated. At the bottom of the tube I made a small hole for the slow subtraction of maple syrup from the container, and for the planned change in the level of satisfaction $\Omega\tau$. If the tube always remains full HR detects that there is no shortage in the level of maple syrup, it does not feel any need, and does not self-activate. As a consequence, it goes on sleeping and does not think. With a programmed loss of maple syrup, the level changes to the point that HR starts to feel an initial state of alert $\pi\nu$. Now it is "aware" that it is the moment to start thinking how to reach again a state of satisfaction $\Omega\tau$. In order to move towards this direction, the whole process of problem-solving is activated. The need, alias the level of maple syrup in the tube, is monitored by a sensor. This sensor, when stimulated, activates HR's internal circuits that were programmed to solve multiple tasks (problem-solving), apart from what is required to bring HR back to the level of need satisfaction $\Omega\tau$. However, if the level of maple syrup decreases up to clear the tube, the need becomes so urgent and predominant that the sensor mechanism—provided with a feedback loop that alerts HR's circuits to refill the tube—will not send signals anymore. It will go off, and the feedback mechanism will fail to refill the tube with maple syrup. The robot breaks down!

It happens also with humans. Children, who receive few positive strokes from their parents, develop a need for love that increases up to a certain point. They continue to seek for love and reassurance from their parents. They "detect" this need for love as their primary life motive. Until they reach a certain threshold, when they no longer hope to receive affection. Here, they seem to give up their pursuit for affection. They seem having developed a containment of their frustration. Love no longer seems important for them. They give up the hope to receive love from their parents. But the model "child" has failed. When adults, these children still seek for love and affection but this awareness is not clear, and all their behaviors are a continuous expression of dependent behaviors that make them seem over-compliant with the wish of other people. Also if this is frustrating, they keep hanging to other people hoping to receive that love they never had from their primary attachment figures. The loss of love represents a kind of lasting urge during their life.

Also our model HR is alive and fully functional, as long as its sensors keep sending impulses to circuits to initiate behaviors useful to satisfy its own needs. But if these behaviors, that are processes of problem-solving, fail to reach their goal, the level of maple syrup reaches the point of no return. At that moment, the "loss" is so severe that the sensor is no acting any more as a feedback mechanism for activating need satisfaction $\Omega\tau$. What happens indeed is that red lights alarm the robot to inform it that it is next to an irreversible damage or, at least, that it is going to be turned off for ever. The loss is irreversible when our robot of first generation can no longer perform the tasks we have programmed in its central panel: washing dishes, cleaning the house, painting the fence. It can no longer self-activate.

Fig. 4.4.1—The simplest mechanism of need detection in a machine.

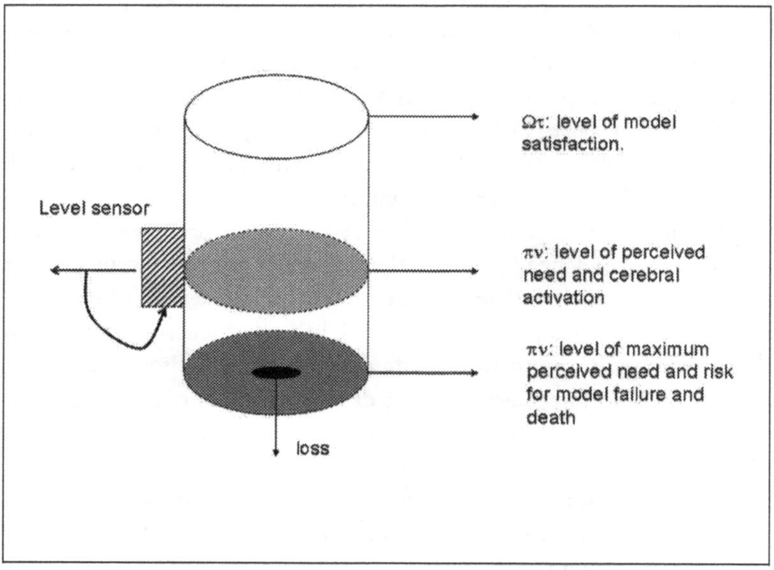

Humans are not different from this mechanism. The central need is usually different: personal growth, need for love, spiritual pursuit, professional advancement, and so on. However, as long as our sensors are active and the model is functional, we are able to reach satisfactory and efficient actions to fulfill these needs. Up to a certain point. If we register only failures, if we always fail professionally, if we cannot obtain the level of love and attachment we feel is important for us, we register a progressive decay in our self-activation. Our actions, that usually serve our mechanisms of problem-solving, become confused and useless. Every order in our thinking seems to proceed randomly. If we are fired from our job, deprived of our daily love, stolen of our money, our inner sensors are in such a state of alert, that is so high and fast, that we register an initial activation of our mental processes for problem-solving. If we are not able to lower this state of alert (by solving these vital problems: job, love, money) then the level of need becomes so predominant that even problem-solving is inhibited, and no productive action is taken anymore. We are now in a state of loss and crisis, and we need psychotherapy to restore our mental functioning. Children in developing countries, who suffer from chronic food deprivation, cannot enter programs for education until their malnutrition is normalized. Without satisfactory levels of daily proteins and vitamins they are underachievers, and learning is too difficult. A progressive apathy ensues, and they fail to flourish.

At this time, we are able to redesign our home robot with more details about how it is conceived.

Fig. 4.4.2—A more "intelligent" mechanism with self-activating strategies when a need is detected.

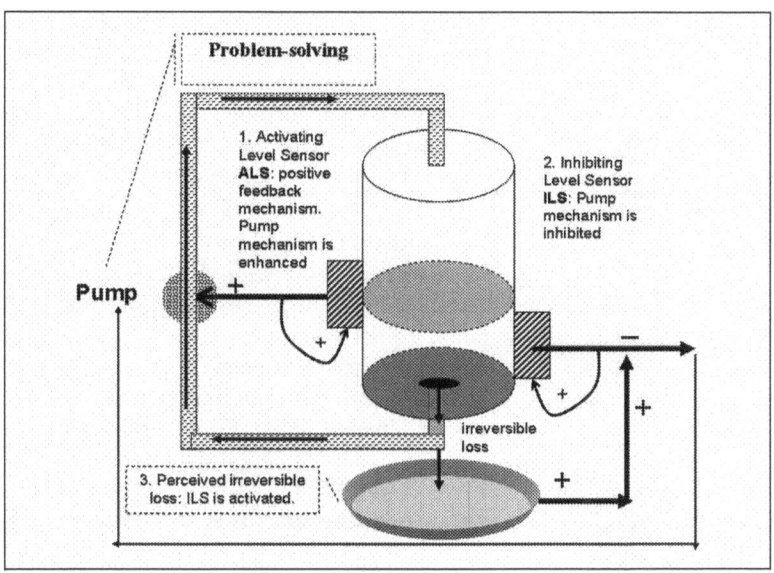

Table 4.4.1—The levels where the sensors are placed depend on our personality. There are many combinations of *ALS* (*Activating Level Sensor*) and *ILS* (*Inhibiting Level Sensor*)

ALS	ILS	Psychology of the person and levels of perceived need πv functional for problem-solving and thinking
Higher level	Bottom level	This person is able to be very sensitive to his/her own needs, and takes soon the lead to solve problems linked to these needs. Stands frustration of low need satisfaction, and does not stop working for final solutions. πv is functional, effective, and activate problem-solving.

ALS	ILS	Psychology of the person and levels of perceived need πv functional for problem-solving and thinking
Medium Level	Medium Level	This person is moderately sensitive to his/her own needs. However, as soon as these needs are perceived, they seem overwhelming and no action is taken to solve relative problems. Many youngsters failing in proper family guidance work with this pattern. Actions are taken with the personal perception that these needs are so profound that no solution is possible. During depression, we assist to the same pattern: helplessness and hopelessness are signs of ILS highly activated. πv is scarcely functional for effective problem-solving.
Bottom Level	Bottom Level	This person has no sensors for his/her own needs. The model is not functional for problem-solving and effective need satisfaction. This person is driven by emotions but is unable to read the status of his own mind. Hypo-Manic people often work according to this level. They seem unaware to recognize their own problems and show morbid processes of problem-solving. There is no πv. Errors are frequent.

Fig. 4.4.3.—The functional diagram for ALS and ILS

High ALS Bottom ILS: πv is functional and effective	Medium ALS Medium ILS: πv is scarcely functional for effective problem-solving.	Bottom ALS, bottom ILS: There is no πv. Errors are frequent.
ALS		
	ALS, ILS	
ILS		ALS, ILS

In this part of the book, we started to familiarize with some important concepts like feedback mechanisms, needs, psychology, etc. This manuscript is structured in a way to give to the reader some basic concepts that would help him/her to familiarize with the way humans as single people, but also as society act, reason, think, feel, behave, etc. We will go back and forth from unity to multitude, from the single person to organization, from mind to machine, from models to practical applications. The effort is to find common descriptions and models that apply to different fields. My personal effort is to read different phenomena with a common frame of reference. My purpose is finally to simplify, as much as possible, the way we can read complex phenomena: thinking, reasoning, problem-solving, psychology and psychopathology. For me, and I hope also for you, it is surprising to find that there are common aspects in different disciplines and common patterns that run across plural facades of human complexity.

4.5. Human complexity

Humans are complex beings. From the previous model, we have seen how a robot can be built in order to have autonomous processes like self-activation to start problem-solving procedures. We have seen that a *need* can function as a prompter of thinking, and that the level of need and need frustration are states that any model detects as a primary concern. Humans do the same. We have basic needs to satisfy. At a certain degree, need satisfaction is an opening for thinking. However, beyond a certain level of needs, these become central and thinking is focused mainly on need satisfaction. Other thoughts become secondary, and there is not much space for being creative. If I know I should soon pay my home bills, I can hardly focus my attention to painting or playing a tune on my piano. Bills become a central need, and the whole process of thinking is on an alert state.

If we are starving, we need food supply and water intake in order to reach again a satisfactory physiological state. As long as primary needs (i.e., love, affection, food, freedom, etc.) are at risk, the only procedures we follow are those concerned with need satisfaction. Often these needs are so rooted that for all our life we invent strategies for need satisfaction. The process of thinking is focused on these needs and their satisfaction, and any other mental process is functional to the fulfilment of these needs. In this instance, problem-solving is directed to reach those targets that are opportune to satisfy the basic need. We seek strokes when we feel a strong need for affection. We think how to escape from a populated city if we feel deprived of our autonomy. We think only to marriage if we perceive our life as meaningful only if we are loved by another human being. During wedding period, the bride is totally focused on the marriage, on the bride dress, on the reception, and nothing else seems to worry her. Other times, we feel quite complete and satisfied with our urges and needs. At this point, we have time to use our brain to concentrate on other different topics for a long period. We start creative mental processes in problem-solving when "our sensors" feel that the level of a basic need is bearable and that we can concentrate on other important issues in our life. For example, it is difficult to find symphony orchestras in developing countries while are focused on starvation or war. Here, some strong urges seem magnetizing minds and wills. On the other side, when our basic needs, such as freedom, food, peace, can find a viable solution, humans become more creative, and schools and universities (where thinking is a basic activity) flourish.

Sometimes, many problem-solving processes can proceed at the same time. Some thoughts are directed to the basic need: it is midday and I'm feel starving. Other may work for other issues: I am preparing budget presentation. Many other processes can focus on inner states: pleasure to work with a nice and sympathetic boss. We can translate this picture of multiple problem-solving processes assigning to each one the following expression:

$$\Omega\tau = \alpha + \tau t_1 + \tau t_2 + \ldots \tau t_n$$

We can further denominate different thought processes with τ_1, τ_2, τ_3, and τ_n, each one fitting the previous expression:

1. $\Omega\tau = \alpha + \tau t_1 + \tau t_2 + \ldots \tau t_n$
2. $\Omega\tau_1 = \alpha + \tau_1 t_1 + \tau_2 t_2 + \ldots \tau_1 t_n$
3. $\Omega\tau_2 = \alpha + \tau_2 t_1 + \tau_2 t_2 + \ldots \tau_2 t_n$
4. Etc.

$$\Sigma\Omega\tau = \Omega\tau_1 + \Omega\tau_2 + \Omega\tau_3 + \Omega\tau_n$$

There are also many needs we should take care of. Our need for protection by living in a safe house and neighborhood. Our need for economic independence by working with a reliable company. Our need for companionship by marrying a loving person. And many others. For each need we activate a train of problem-solving processes in order to lower the level of need activation and to reach a solution or acceptable satisfaction $\Omega\tau$: a house with a nice garden in a green environment; a contract with our company; the love of our husband or wife; etc. What we find is that needs are interrelated, and processes of problem-solving often overlap. I am not fully satisfied if I am not able to find a nice house in a wood, if I cannot live there with the person I love most, and employed in a close company not far from where I live. These things have for me the same priority. Consequently, when I think about a solution, I usually prefer to find one that fits all these aspects. Explaining this last concept with set theory, we see that the sets identified by τ_1, τ_2, τ_3, overlap, at least in the area (blacken in the next figure) where I consider these needs as equally important. The darken area, or common need $\chi\nu$ (Greek initials for "C", common, and "N", need) is expressed in set theory as:

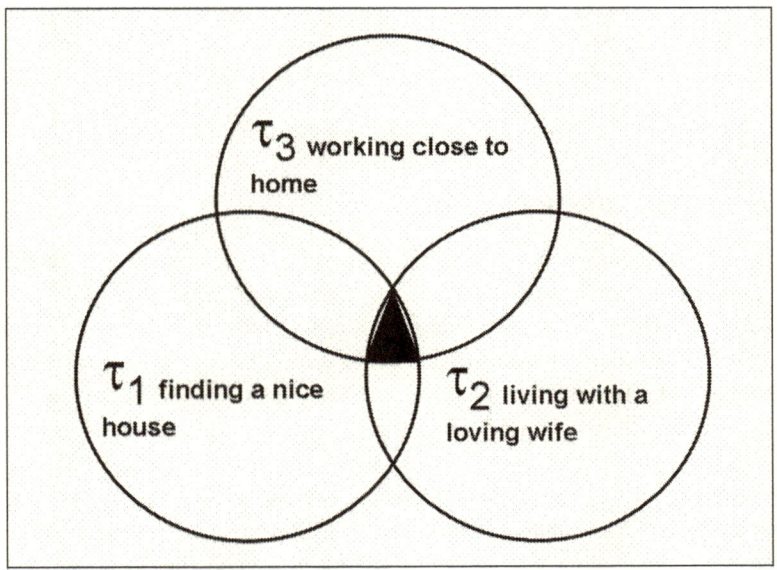

$$\chi\nu = \tau_1 \cap \tau_2 \cap \tau_3$$

Even the final solution can be the end result of any single solution for each thought process. For example. If I move to a big city it is easier to find a nice job, to earn enough money to buy a splendid house, and become an attractive party for pretty women. This satisfying end solution $\chi\Omega$ is the overlap of each single solution:

$$\chi\Omega = \chi\Omega\tau t_1 \cap \chi\Omega\tau t_2 \cap \chi\Omega\tau t_3$$

However, as we know, not always our dreams work. There is something that goes wrong with our programs, and we fail to reach our final goal. This multiple-step solution often appears much more complex than step-by-step solutions. Perhaps the error ε increases with the number of single problem-solving processes we add up with similar ones. The largest the number N of problems P we have to solve *at the same time*, the higher the probability p of committing errors ε and of missing our target:

$$p\varepsilon \propto NP$$

Therefore, the probability of making errors in processes of problem-solving is directly proportional to the number of single problems we are trying to solve to reach a final target solution. Any single problem is represented by a chain of thought-processes that are activated to solve a single need.

4.6. Practice and habituation

Practice makes people more experts in problem-solving and pattern recognition. This means that the process of problem-solving applied at the same problem many times a day, will decrease the number of errors ε, and will increase the probability of successes in problem resolution. Another consequence in repeating the same strategies to solve the same problem is that the whole process becomes more and more automatic. Given a certain amount of time, problem resolution becomes automatic, and the awareness of each single step needed to solve the problem becomes ingrained in our subconscious mechanisms. Driving a care for those who got a driver license many years ago is simpler compared to what is required to those who just passed the driving examination. For the first expert drivers, each single step (moving the shift, steering the wheel, pushing the brake, etc.) is so automatic that they scarcely pay an active attention to each single action. Therefore problem-solving is directly proportional to time T.

$$\tau \propto T$$

Another consequence is that exact (unmistaken) solutions increase in frequency with repetition of strategies of problem-solving, while errors decrease.

$$\chi\Omega \Leftarrow +\Delta T$$

The previous expression tells us that *the increase of time spent in processes of problem-solving also increases the probability of satisfying solutions to each single problem. Practice increases the probability of a satisfying problem solution.*

$$\Delta T / \varepsilon = k$$

The previous expression tells us that *the number errors are inversely proportional to the time employed to repeat the process activated for the solution of the same problem. Practice decreases the probability of making final errors during the application of the same processes of problem-solving. The more we practice the less errors we make.*

The probability of success is very high in mankind. An amoeba and many inferior species of animals fail to learn from experience, and easily die because did not apply the same procedures for the solution of similar problems. Therefore, the probability of success $p\sigma$ (Greek "p" and "s") is directly proportional to the "smartness of the model". There are some people, however, who do not learn from experience. They lack in self confidence, and consider any problem as different from any similar one. In this case, they spend a lot of energy to find new solutions when they already have them. A basic attitude to catastrophize in depressed people make them less confident in their capabilities to the point that a lot of psychic energy is spend to find new solutions to old problems. On the other hand, people with Obsessive Compulsive Disorder (OCD) stick to the same procedures in an obsessive way, and repeat each time the whole process compulsively. Even if the problem slightly changes they are unable to change a familiar pattern. Therefore, they use old strategies for new problems, and easy decisions are difficult. Both depressive and obsessive-compulsive people have internal self-defeating models for problem solving. The probability of success $p\sigma$ is very low, while the probability of errors $p\varepsilon$ very high. This is one of the reasons why it is a primary goal to help them to overcome ineffective cognitive schemes before helping them in new problem-solving strategies. Here, again, we find the influence of emotions on problem-solving, and we can imagine that $p\sigma$ and $p\varepsilon$ are subsets of the emotional domain.

4.7. About unexpected events and learning

Problem solution is under our control but unpredictable events altering the process of problem-solving are not. Therefore, in our calculation of factors involved in the final solution of a problem, we should imagine unpredictable events as always being present at the beginning as unknown factors or during the process of problem-solving as intervening unknown factors.

Unknown factors are often referred as variables, but the denomination is not simple because:

- The characteristic of the intervening unknown factors is unknown per se.
- The time of intervention is also unknown.
- The effect on the whole process of problem-solution of the unknown variable is not verifiable.

However, everyday we make difficult decisions also with the sense that some unknown variable could interfere with the process and even with the solution. Our program for a nice week-end on the mountains to fish, could be interrupted by a bad thunderstorm. However, we cannot control the unpredictability. And unpredictability itself gives a flavour to our life. One day, while I decided that a girl would have replied "no" to my invitation to a pizza party, she answered "yes". Thus, mystery is an invitation to use our brain to predict what is unknown. Furthermore, people can be distinguished as wise as long as they consider unpredictability as an intervening factor with a high probability. However, no matter when the mystery of our life will meet us, we do not know two things: *what* the mystery is and *when* we will meet it.

Let us name with "υ" the unpredictable factor, that is, the *what*, the *when* it will appear to influence our problem-solving. Unpredictability is always a matter of time T applied to the *unknown* υ, that is υT. The equation for problem-solving including the unknown υ will then become:

$$\Omega\tau = [\alpha + \tau t_1 + \tau t_2 + \dots \tau t_n] + [x\,\upsilon T]$$

I have put x before the unknown factor because we cannot predict how many times it will intervene to influence problem-solving. However, we should not think of υT as a negative factor. Many important discoveries and inventions were made because of unpredictable factors intervening in a problem that seemed not giving any solution by treating it with usual strategies. Wisdom is not a matter of forgetting $x\upsilon T$. Indeed, we show flexible thinking when we take into account the chances of meeting unpredictability. A company that produces goods, and that is not keeping an eye on the time factor T of $x\upsilon T$ (i.e., loss of market for the outfit at time T1 or T2) is at risk for accumulation of goods in the production plants without any chance to sell the supplementary stock. Impulsive people, with borderline traits, usually do not learn from experience. They show some difficulty in predicting or even in understanding the existence of υT in their life. They seem to treat unexpected facts as absolutely foreign to their life. On the other hand, obsessive-compulsive people seem to be glued on their decisional processes because they are over-evaluating $x\upsilon T$. They never risk in making also simple decisions. As a result, they never arrive to a final and easy decision.

Guiding a space craft into a comet would be almost impossible without giving a mature importance to $x\upsilon T$. Decisional processes, either human or cybernetic, must included *loops* that go back and forth from a known procedure, to a new immediate course that includes any new variables $x\upsilon T$ as part participant in the whole problem-solving equation. This self-adjustment process is natural in biological models that are considered by system theories as "open" because able to adjust to variations in environment, that is, the to the occurrence of $x\upsilon T$. If we want to build a self-adjusting model, for example a home robot that can cook for us, or if we want to help an obsessive friend, we should teach them to consider $x\upsilon T$. Namely, what they need, is a series of recursive equations of problem-solving, progressively including $x\upsilon$ (Fig. 4.7.1.).

If I am invited to a barbeque on a Sunday at the home of my girlfriend with her parents, I feel that I can fill my backpack with a stock of unpredictable factors υ. My problem-solving process, alias, my mind, because my heart is so involved, will have some difficulty in being clear. Any time, I have to enclose into my thought processes new variables: parents of my girlfriend, her brother who is a foot-ball player, her dangerous dog, and many others. All this demands a continuous adjustment of my thinking. The same happens in the brave pilot who is guiding his space craft in the tale of a comet. The equations in his mind and in his computer would treat the variables υ "almost" in the same way they treat known variables. We start from what we have! But most important, at time $(T + \mu T)$, just a fraction of seconds after we have met the unpredictable fact, it becomes a piece of experience in our mind and in our model. We start to learn from experience very soon. This is a gift that human beings have. Children have more, but also many adults. *We know that we learn from experience. This is a fact we find in many books. But any experience was an unknown variable just few seconds before we met it, that is, at time* $(T - \mu T)$.

Fig. 4.7.1—Recursive problem-solving processes including several unpredictability $x\upsilon$T.

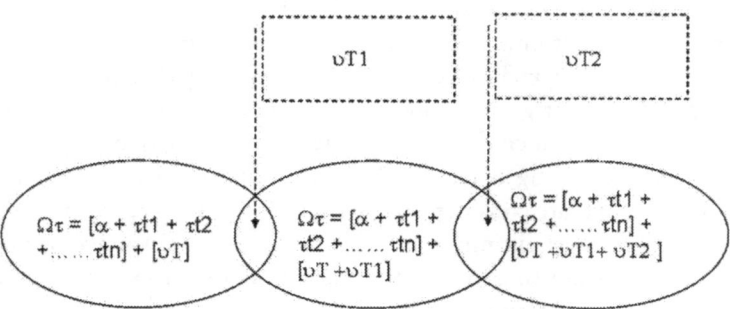

If we want to express this concept in another way, we can say that: *learning is a way we keep into consideration and treat unexpected events in our life. Using thought processes able to treat previous unexpected events as a new experience is at the basis of learning in human models.*

In the following table we will consider how people with different personalities treat the events when they still seem unpredictable [υ (T − μT)], and when they can become a piece of personal experience [υ (T + μT)]:

Table 4.7.1—Personality and problem-solving strategies applied to unpredictability.

Personality	Way to consider unpredictability [υ (T − μT)]	Way to consider experience and learning [υ (T + μT)]
Borderline personality	They have grown in families "soap operas". Unpredictability was the common experience. They never made experience of trusting events because they were always "threatening" and unknown.	They have not enough trust in events although they experience some familiarity and goodness in the experience itself. Therefore, thinking is hindered by fear of the unknown, while trust in events is mirrored by the behavior of important others coping with the same events.
Depressive personality	Since infancy, they familiarized with negative events. In their personal experience, unpredictable losses outnumbered positive life experiences. What is unpredictable is often sad and carries negative feelings.	Their cognitive scheme, reinforced by multiple losses, leads them to be familiar only with negative life events. Positive facts and experiences are not on the same wave length of what they think about life. Thinking is possible but the fear for future and unpredictability slows down their drive for experiencing new events.

Personality	Way to consider unpredictability [υ (T – μT)]	Way to consider experience and learning [υ (T + μT)]
Paranoid personality	The hallmark in their thinking is that everything is unpredictable. They treat at the same way known and unknown events. Mistrust is a matter of rejecting data from experience (predictable facts) as if they were carrying some unknown quality (that is, are unpredictable threats). Their suspiciousness is a consequence of a process of mistrusting their own thinking and problem-solution.	Thinking may appear brilliant. But the basic aspect is that even if they become familiar with some aspect of life, they always suspect that they have missed something in their evaluation. A paranoid person is happy only when s/he has found "evidence" that his/her positive thinking about a person or a fact was indeed faulty, and he can gather new evidence supporting new persecutory considerations about the same person or fact. Their suspects can be finally confirmed.
Obsessive-compulsive personality	More than anyone else, obsessive thought is characterized by a continuous concentration on details. These people mostly come from families where there is an emphasis to perfection, performance and hatred for mistakes. As a consequence, unpredictability, an unwanted threat, forces them to spend a substantial time of their lives to reduce to zero the chances that unpredictable events may indeed occur. Nevertheless, in a healthy personality, a mean amount in obsessive thinking is needed to master environments and data that are unfamiliar, polymorphic, and dangerous. Thought process, when activated for problem-solving, has a continuous rehearsal of future scenes. Machines that work according to this process, are often life-saving and are used to make predictions of future events	Experience and learning are welcomed as factors that increase predictability. However, this is a laborious process, and requires a continuous control over thought processes. On the other hand, if this is problematic for humans, in complex robots, obsessive learning and over-rehearsal will reduce chances for mistakes and will enhance the processes for which the machine is designed. Learning machine use old and new data to self-adjust by looping.

4.8. How to visualize the process of thinking

We can illustrate with some lines in a Cartesian box how the function of thinking would look like. In both cases the lines of the function never cross the value of 0 because we can imagine that we never start from a vacuum: there is always a hint of thought that is the catalyst for the process that follows. In the figure, the line for the function $[F(y) = x+1x+2x+3x]$ is not straight although made by equal amounts of thoughts unit x. The unknown y simply represents the final thought that in another part of the book we have represented by Ω. Time factor t is withdrawn because according to the unit chosen (seconds, minutes, hours) it is meant to be the same (1sec. 1 min., 1 hour, etc) in any thought shot $(x+x_n)$ in any given function. This function simply means that in order to arrive to a final thought y about a matter, I add up chokes that are similar unit of simple thoughts x. For example in order to be able to meet the parents of my girlfriend that has invited me to a barbeque, I buy some flowers, then I go to the barber, then I rehearse how I will introduce myself, etc.

The final curve shows an increase that is progressive in this graphic but, as we can soon see, it does not reach an infinite value. Therefore, the curve becomes horizontal at a certain point. If it strives to reach an infinite value ∞ my thinking would never stops. It means that I feel that there is always something missing that is needed to reach the perfection or mathematical infinity ∞. No matter how ready I am to meet my girlfriend's parents, there is always something I feel is missing. Many obsessive people fall in this loop as if the curve were perfect by reaching an ideal maximum value ∞.

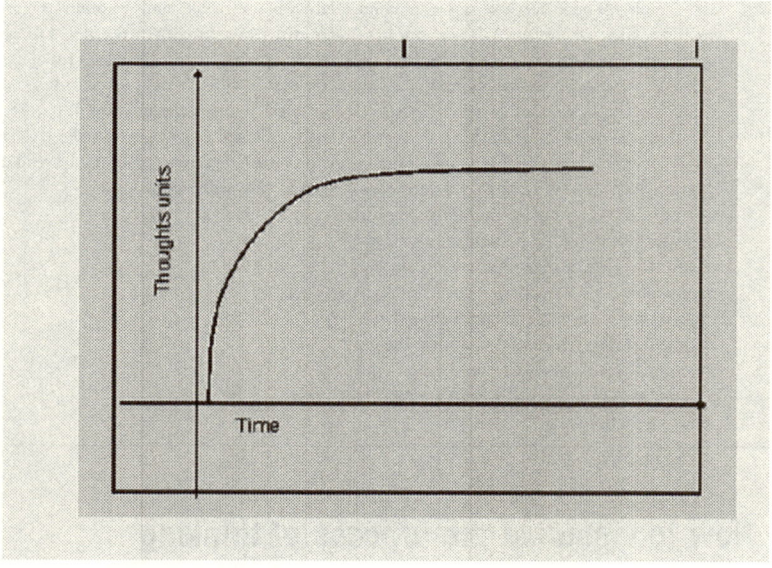

If I am dressing properly to go to the house of my girlfriend for a barbeque, and I am deciding what to dress, the problem is falling in a loop that makes decision impossible because I think that perfection is possible and that, given enough time, the final decision y can have its maximum value, that is, it can reach ∞. Thoughts serve to make decisions. Thinking per se is pure philosophy which is not where we are aiming to with this book. A more natural curve that will help me to dress properly for the meeting of my girlfriend's parents is the logarithmic one (C shaped) where the y axis is for the units of thoughts (or bits of problem-solving), and the *x* axis represents the passage of time in the unit we have chosen (seconds, minutes, hours).

4.9. How to measure thought units

When I am thinking what to dress in order to go out for a dinner with the most beautiful girl of the college the final decision is not easy. I must chose the dress, the shirt, the pants, the shoes, the hear cut, etc. However, any of these things has a name, and its name is selected amongst other names. Let us make that the final decision is:

"Black Shoes, White Shirt, Blue Jeans, Dark Jacket"

Or in symbolic model from the initials:

BS+WS+BJ+DJ

Where:

BS = x_1, WS = x_2; BJ = x_3, DJ = x_4

Each unknown is a bit of thought of the final decision "Dress for this evening" or *y*. But what is the size of *x*? If we think to an analogical model, in my mind, "Black Shoes" is composed by 10 characters. Even if I symbolize it with BS in my mind I have or a noun "Black Shoes" or the image of Black Shoes. If I think in a digital way I have only 1 noun and 1 adjective. For example a frame 00011000, or two bits, or in a WORD document 20K. I like this last solution because it is more familiar. For example, I have calculated that my work, mostly (not always spent by thinking and writing what I think) could fill a 1 Gigabyte memory of my memory card. This seems an attractive solution also because figures (images) occupy more space than just words. However, in many people, recalling images is a mnemonic trick that works well. We have a capable brain. It does not matter at the moment if the word "Back Shoes" occupies 20Kb of my brain or its image 200Mb. We have internal compressors that work in a wonderful way!!! So, if we put "bites" as unit of thinking, by counting on our WORD processor the word "BS+WS+BJ+DJ" we get 20 KB.

Finally, I conclude that in order to be properly dressed for meeting my girlfriend in a restaurant I need to ask to my brain to produce 20KB of information. Or, F(*y*) = 20KB which is 8 words in 42 characters. Writing a letter to my girlfriend is more complex. I am unveiling things of my life. Perhaps, if I count what that writing has occupied on my computer, I reach some mega-bites of memory, and I would fill all my memory-card! In this sense, if we adopt bytes as though units, any complete thought is given by a sum of byte/time unit and in the Cartesian box: y is "byte" while x is "seconds". Moreover, if I employing a week to decide what to dress that magic night the amount of thinking does not change, it is still 20 KB. But the speed of my thinking is determined by the time factor and the whole decision, this time, was 20KB/1 week. This is the final thought of many decisions, and it could be probable that I have selected thousands of options. This means that "20KB/1 week" is the final result of 1MB thoughts per day. And so on. Both are thinking process but we know that in order to make a good decision we cannot think for the eternity: time factor cannot be infinite ∞. But we also know that we cannot dress 20 shirts, or 10 jackets at the same moment. All I can dress is 20 KB of nice dress coming out of a monumental 1 GB of other options! Therefore, from the fountain pours 1 MB of fresh thought any hour, and from here, I collect 20 KB of ideas in order to dress for the meeting with my girlfriend! Eighty KB where discharged as non important for my choice. However, at the end, I have thought for a total amount of 1 MB in order to have 20 KB.

Obsessive people who take into account any option are not synthetic. People with a good self-esteem reach a rapid solution with a lesser use of bites. Perhaps they reach a 20 KB decision out of 40 KB. An obsessive reaches 20 KB decision out of 1 MB. And, perhaps the rate for depressive people is 10 KB out of 10 KB: everything seems so important that due to a process of thinking, called generalization, they do not like to miss fringe information afraid to leave out important things. In addition, they do not incorporate much information because they easily become tired in thinking. We can think about different patterns of thinking if we use the ratio y/x^n where "y" is the final thought or decision, while "x^n" are the units of thoughts needed to reach y, and the exponent "n" is the number of these operations. Anyone is characterized by a y/x^n ratio that in some extents predicts characteristic patterns for each personality.

Table 4.9.1—The table shows how we think according to data available. In the ratio y/x^n, "y" is the final thought or decision, while "x^n" are the units of thoughts needed to reach y. Finally, "n" is the number of these operations.

y/x^n ratio	*Meaning*	*Personality trait*	*Cognitive Therapy*
< 1	This is the normal process of decision making where the person is using a selection (y) of options (x^n) to reach a final decision. Here $y < x^n$.	Normal	None
> 1	It means that a person is using more elements than are really present. On the basis of few options, the decision is richer than the known or viable variables. Here $y > x^n$.	Creative but also ipomanic personalities who decide on the basis of a scarce number of known variables.	Reality test. Ipomanic must know that decisions that carry more variables than those really present can lead to faulty thoughts: i.e. buying a car without having verified the sum available in their bank account.
= 1	It means that a person makes a decision carrying the same complexity of the know variables needed to decide. Usually few options are available. Here $y = x^n$.	Depressed people use all the viable options for problem solving. The same applies to obsessive people: everything seems so important to be discharged.	These people should accept indeterminacy and decisions based on few available options. It is not important to grasp the whole universe to make good guessing.

4.10. A cerebral pacemaker

To summarize, we shall consider mind as a system that decodes and encodes messages from environment, and transforms them into thoughts and behaviors. No matter how different and complex inputs and outputs are, mind always transforms them into states of neuronal excitement and rest, classifiable as ON-OFF states or "1-0" status according to an analogical model. Even outputs, in the form of thoughts, are messages decoded by an array or set of neurones in an "ON-OFF" state. In addition, we should imagine that any unbiased (healthy) idea abut self, others and world, is a message with a high degree of semantic complexity, and *this complexity decreases with the increase in the severity of mind pathologies (either psychic or physical)*. If I think of my girlfriend simply as a "pretty" girl, my mind is simplifying a person who is also "excellent, intelligent, sensitive, empathic". In a simplified concept, the amount of information about a person or object will decrease while the entropy (a cybernetic concept to indicate a degree of mess) will increase. Complexity in thoughts is differentiated according to the *amount* of neuronal subsystems acting. Perhaps, I am not using all my cerebral neurons to classify my girlfriend: I am oversimplifying! Neurons, and therefore, mental processes, can be functionally impaired, physiological impaired (i.e., I am sleepy), or altered by environmental (too much noise to think clearly) or neurochemical (I am starving) factors.

Our theory would not be complete if we do not consider in the mind the existence of a "*cerebral pacemaker*" (CP) that acts as a functional area that is self-activated[11]. It works as the manager of our mind. In other words, it starts the different processes of thinking, the direction of which is determined only during a second time. In other words, it is the "START!" signal that switches on the whole process of thinking.

CP activates mental processes, and *very shortly, but always, comes before any thought process.* Depending on the complexity of the task, it is partly or totally activated. According to a semantic and functional classification, the activity of the CP may be subdivided as in the table, for example, for the task: "Buying flowers to my girlfriend":

- *General Activation of Thinking (GAT): is resumed by the word: "Let's think!".*
- *General Categorical Activation of Thinking (GCAT): "Let's think about flowers to buy!".*
- *Selected Categorical Activation of Thinking (SCAT): "Let's think about roses!".*
- *Selected Activation of Thinking (SAT): "Let's think about a violet rose!".*
- *Selected Activation of Thinking from Long Term Memory (SATLTM): "Let's think about that rose I saw the other day!".*
- *Selected Activation of Thinking from Attention (SATA): "Let's think about that flower I am seeing!".*
- *General Activation of Thinking from Creativity (GATC): "Let's think about a new flower I can create in my garden!".*

We should also notice that people with severe neurotic problems such as phobia, hypochondria, or obsessive-compulsive disorders, in a certain way, show over activation of some of these categories. In a certain way, we find a prevalence of the Selected Categorical Activation to the detriment of the more general activation of thinking (Cannot see the forest around the tree).

5 Understanding thought disorders

5.1. Introduction

This part of the book aims to describe models to understand the origin and development of psychological problems. A particular emphasis is given to several approaches that allow an inference on how man elaborates inputs from environment in order to form ideas, feelings and thoughts. A symbolic logic approach is also considered. Finally, psychotherapeutic interventions are considered as they relate to the model developed.

My model considers how to elucidate mind functions during psychopathological disorders[12,13]. Organic, affective, and personality pathologies, and other psychopathological illnesses, make the main focus of psychologists, psychotherapists, and neuroscientists. My aim was to find a cybernetic model which could be used to explain the dynamics that link organic impairments to thought and affective disorders. In its basic assumption, cybernetics means "governor". Wiener also considers mind as a digital machine working on all-or-nothing basis[14]. It is interesting to note that pathological thought contents could be considered as a minus process where the impairment of some neuronal networks and the absence of negative feed-back mechanisms will assure the perpetuation of the observed disorder. The person and his mind are unable to work as an open system (adopting a Bertalanffy terminology) and, consequently, to change the course of thinking. In other words, this person has problems in adopting signals coming from the world (input feed-back) and reality in order to adjust the train of thinking accordingly to reality test. I also adopted a systemic model to explain the complexity in the structure of mind. Moreover, this model could either be referred to as a neuronal network or a set of cerebral centers which transcend the cellular component. Therefore mind has a structure based on a set of neurons or functional centers, with a complexity arranged according to a network model. In addition, we shall consider any psychopathological thought disorder as a minus process, mainly based on an *increased* number of malfunctioning neuronal centers, or neuronal pathways (such as, the serotoninergic pathways for depression) in an OFF state. Even when no neuroanatomical basis can be found, the inner structure of affective, psychotic or neurotic disorders, as they are evidenced during psychotherapy, show that the person and his mind are *closed* to outer influences, are unable to adjust to inputs from outside in order to make a complete reality test, and, consequently, cannot learn from experience. What are more important are the *quantitative* aspects given to this theory according to which the structure of mind and thinking is not based on a vacuum, on an unknown secret limbo where nobody should inquire. Indeed, with some complex passage, I would like to suggest that mind should be considered as a *transformer* that is, it receives inputs that are of different origin (neurochemical, sensory, physical, electric, psychological, social, etc.) but that are all translated in states of excitement of particular sets of neurons, and finally transformed into thoughts, emotions, and actions. Even in people not suffering from any psychopathology, we could identify a set of statements which characterize the way in which that person sees reality: knowledge, prejudices, past experiences. Theories of logic could help us to understand how inputs of reality are elaborated by a subject in behaviors and thoughts which make the final mind output.

5.2. Complexity and uniqueness

From a psychological point of view, the concept of homeostasis is important in understanding the model. In addition, although the uniqueness of any human being should always be underlined, some emotional answers are more predictable and stereotypical compared to the infinite number of inputs that a person receives during his or her own life. The fact that we can make predictable explanations would be contradictory if we affirm that anyone is unique in his way of reacting to reality and forming emotions. If this were so, fields like psychology and sociology would not exist. However, within some range of mistakes, it is always possible to construct a *map* (usually identified as categories) of mental schemes, classified on the basis of some similarities, and thus clearly distinguishable amongst them. Today, saying that a person is depressed, manic, paranoiac, etc., easily drives the attention to standard behaviors. But strangely enough, these clear classifications would be weak if we adhere to the thesis that states that any human mind is different from any other in every person on Earth. However, complexity and uniqueness are always assured, although we know that any human brain has the same structures in everybody. Trans-cultural psychiatry has shown that depression and depressive behavior are the same in every man on Earth and that, within a certain range of differences, we can classify certain behaviors as paranoiac, manic, delusional, etc. This would not be possible if, at the basis of depression, paranoia, delusion, etc., are not the same processes. *That is to say that, accepting the uniqueness of man, thoughts and emotions are caused by the same processes, and are equal in any man.* Therefore, although everyone is different from others on the basis of his own history, birth, social influences, genetic structure, his/her brain responds to different inputs in the same way. However, the outputs, such as thoughts and emotions, are different depending on the prevailing cognitive-emotional scheme. Therefore, we are more similar than we thought, and even if I feel mildly depressed because I could not eat my daily portion of milk chocolate, and even if you are depressed because your girlfriend or boyfriend could not come with you to watch a movie, our minds are depressed at the same way and in a similar manner. Here, causes change (inputs) and not the effects (outputs as ideas and thoughts). In this case, reasons are biochemical as concerning chocolate, psychological as concerning the missed appointment. From here on, our brain will elaborate these different inputs in the same fashion, first transforming these experiences into neuronal excitation (ON) or rest (OFF), and then selecting a set of *boxes* (here, functional units using the same logic predicates) that, taken together in a certain way, output the resulting emotion: depression. Thus, if we both feel depressed (output) it means that the set of boxes (or functional units related to specific cognitive outputs) in our brains that are ON are those that output: "feeling down", "being pessimistic", "having a low self-esteem", and so on. Saying the same into logic statements, it means that the system mind is "tuned" according to a certain set of possibilities in examining "statements" from reality. These statements correspond to almost any of the expressions in symbolic logic [∧ (*et*) and, ∨ *(vel)* or, ⊃ (if then), etc.]. I suspect that any morbid affective state is a *minus process* whereas in a *normal thinking usually there is no prevalence of sets* in a *on* or *off* state at the poles of a continuum where in between we place what sounds to be a *normal* thought. For example, the continuum depression/mania for affective disorders, or the continuum inward/outward looking for obsessive people, etc. Therefore, if one pole of the continuum is more active because the set that is an ON state prevails, or because the other pole is affected by a cerebral pathology so that its function is impaired, we have then a certain mood state, an ideation, a behavior, a way of seeing reality, each one making the *output.*

Another characteristic of mental processes is the low or high receptivity to external factors: social, psychological, biochemical, etc. That is, in some case, mind acts as a closed system, that is, it not responsive to healing inputs or data that come from reality or psychotherapy: the system-mind does not change its cognitive schemes.

Indeed, I suggest that psychotherapy and psychoactive drugs act on the same cerebral neuronal systems, to determine outputs (emotions) of the same quality but of different intensity. What we do with this model is to change a qualitative (psychotherapy versus pharmacological) difference into a quantitative explanation:

strength in activating (or inactivating) some center in an OFF/ON state. Kramer (1993)[15] has been able to suggest that even the kind of words that a psychotherapist says to his depressed patients might be imagined as determining biological changes in the mind of his patient in the same way (but with a different intensity) as an antidepressant does. The change of hypochondriac ideation after a few weeks of treatment with the antidepressant drug Fluoxetine is more rapid and efficacious than only psychotherapy. By using psychopharmacology and psychotherapy, the hypochondriac person becomes more open to alternatives and less concentrated on somatic discomforts.

The quality of the input does not change the characteristics of the selector, our mind. No matter how different inputs are, they are always elaborated as neuronal states of excitement, and finally translated in a number of neurons in an ON or OFF state. For example, if we indicate with "1" the neurons in an ON state, and with "0" the neurons in an OFF state, we are able to say that the concept "outlook of life", has a state of excitement characterized by "111101" for an optimistic outlook of life, and "000010" for a pessimistic one.

We shall think that any psychopathology makes mind more similar to a closed system than to an open one. It is always a minus process, while mind self-maintains its state of deviation. The psychopathology, present in an affective or a personality disorders, is a characteristic of closed systems where mind does not respond to inputs either from outside, that is, reality, or from inside, self-perception. A closed system is also biased, and *pathological though disorders* are not a qualitative attribute but a quantitative process wherein some sets of cognitive schemes are prevailing on one of the two poles of a continuum (not necessarily, bidimensional).

5.3. Making inferences about systems

The way we generate concepts and ideas much depends on the mental processes we use to treat data from reality. Basically we can distinguish two broad categories of people, depending on their way to generate ideas: the simplifier and the analytic.

The simplifier.—There are people (and systems) that react in the same way no matter what the inputs are. In addition, incoming information, although different, usually generate the same behavioral answers, ideas, thoughts, etc. There are some persons who would say: "People are selfish!". They would make this assumption for anyone: for the youngest people or for the oldest people, for a clergyman or for a thief, for a man or for a woman, for a European or for a North American, etc. This way of processing information could be simplified by assigning a letter to any input: Y (the youngest), O (the oldest), C (clergyman), T (thief), M (man), and W (woman). Then, a simplification is expressed by a mathematical expression where: Y = O = C = T = M = W. Usually, low caps letters are used, so our expression would become: $[p = q = r = s = t = u]$. The simplifier also simplifies reality. However, simplification could be the best fit in a complex environment that changes continuously. Here, a fine discrimination would lower adaptation or predictions. However, it is more frequent in depressed people or lowly aroused persons. From one statement they predict others. This way of reasoning is also called "common sense". In a certain way, this would allow a system to adapt even if cognitive complexity cannot be assured. To summarize, a $[p = q = r = s = t = u]$ system: i) is a low complexity system; ii) elaborates information at a high speed but with a low fine discrimination; iii) usually it is structurally simple and responds by ON-OFF states, that is, it reacts or not to the input (e.g., a light switch will open no matter how strong is the force we use to push it; in some extent, it does not make a fine discrimination of the strength used to turn it on; a switch button works, or does not work, depending on the fact that we push it or not; etc.); iv) therefore, inputs are elaborated in the same way; v) there is a "centrifugal" analysis of stimuli: from particular to general ("they can see the wood but not the tree"). Simplification is a way of economically coping with reality.

The analytic.—Mind can react in a different way to environmental stimuli. Each input determines one and only one output (behavior, thought, action, etc.). Coming back to our example "People are selfish!", the analytic person would make a discrimination based, perhaps, on personal experiences: $[p \neq q \neq r \neq s \neq t \neq u]$. These are creative and analytic people. However, obsessive people too, would make very fine discriminations of inputs. This way of examining reality could be the best fit in a predictable environment which does not change very often. However, cognitive complexity hinders an economic way of coping with reality. In these analytic persons, one statement (input) would not predict its conclusions (output). A prevailing analytic attitude is a characteristic of highly aroused people, obsessive people, anxious, neurotics, and hypochondriacs. Characteristics of the analytic system is: i) to be a complex system; ii) usually it works on a "continuum" (e.g., a cursor for the volume of a stereo, an amplifier, etc.); iii) inputs are elaborated in a different way; iv) there is a "centripetal" analysis of stimuli: from general to particular ("they can see the tree but not the wood"). Cognitive complexity is an expensive way to analyze data but increases creativity and problem solving strategies. However, in OCD (obsessive-compulsive disorders) a person is self-centered and unable to "take things easily".

Nevertheless, one person could change from one mental scheme to another one, from being a simplifier to being an analytic according to the moment, to reality exigency, to life experiences, to mood state, to psychotherapeutic interventions, etc. People and systems continuously adapt to environmental losses and gains, and without a basic substrate (or core identity) they would change too rapidly. Identity is a strategy for adapting to environment in a way that adjustment to changing stimuli is possible and not traumatic. *Identity is not a static mental state unchanged by stimuli but a dynamic mechanism where a person continuously strives to maintain the "same" self.* We change enormously during a twenty-four hour period. How we feel in the morning is very different from how we feel at night in the same day. An infinite number of environmental stimuli (work problems, the quality in our marital relationship, the economic future of our country, social problems, even our car not working properly) are always challenging our self-unity. We all adapt to our changing environment, to losses, stresses, inputs, information, etc. But adaptation also influences our identity. A sudden loss is enough to make us feel depressed and low spirited. We feel as not being the same. Something has changed. There is not such a thing like a "solid" character, personality or feeling. We all adapt. Therefore, in some extent, adapting organisms and systems are *psycho-dynamic* and not *psycho-static*. Therefore, a feeling derives from an "average" of fluctuating emotions. At the same time, psychopathology is a way of psychostatically approaching reality, which means being low in mental strategies that help in coping with a dynamic reality. In some extent, *a dynamic and cybernetic approach to psychopathology is any intervention which would act on inputs in order to change mind from being a closed (and less dynamic) to being an open (and more dynamic state) system.* In other words, psychotherapy is made by "mind-opening" strategies like words, psychoactive drugs (antidepressants, antipsychotic, anti-anxiety) or behaviors (a simple kiss and a hug could adjust a broken love).

5.4. Psychotherapeutic interventions

In any open system, logic categories ($p \wedge q$, $p \vee q$, $p \supset q$, etc.) could change according to requirements of adaptation, and reality test. Another characteristic of biased cognitive schemes is the low or high influence by *some* external input: social, psychological, biochemical, and so on. That is, in some case, mind acts as a closed system. In this case, reality or psychotherapy, although acting as positive force addressed from the therapist to the patient in order to lower the intensity of his/her problem, will not influence the course of thinking: this person does not change his or her internal status and keeps using the same old strategies to master new problems. Even in *normal thinking* strong prejudices and discrimination could exert the same effect according to how the **logic system of interpretation** (LSI) in mind ($\wedge$ [and], $\vee$ [or], $\supset$ [if then], etc.) works. In other cases, a combined therapy (psychotherapy plus psychopharmacology) seems acting more intensely. In this sense, any psychotherapeutic intervention integrating counseling, psychotherapy, behavioral therapy, spiritual care, acts by changing the prevailing thought processes, and by helping a person to use a wide range of problem solving strategies to master internal conflicts. In cases of severe crises, it is more difficult to change old strategies. Mind reacts by using what it already knows. In other words, it behaves as a closed systems where more and more sets do not respond to feedback input either from outside reality, or from inside, that is, the internal feedback or insight. A closed system is also biased, and it cannot change its LSI. In this case, *our mind is adopting cognitive schemes, corresponding to logic operations* (and, or, if then, etc.), *that are less effective for successfully coping with reality.* What happens is that inputs from reality encounter logic filters that treat these data with expensive mental strategies. It is like to enter the front door of our garage by using a truck instead of a reasonable car. We loose in efficiency and gain in stress and depression because at the moment we are making tremendous efforts to master simple problems.

5.5. Psycho-openness

Anyone is familiar with that particular taste that life assumes when we are in a bad mood. Everything seems grey and pleasure seems gone away forever. Even simple stimuli change their familiar attributes: smell, taste, and ear. We can say that the world has lost his poetry. Well, our mind is very sensitive to mood states, and the same applies to our thought processes. Our mental neurons are not simple robots that send neurochemical signals when they like. They also are "sensitive" through axonal connections to our feelings in a mutual influence. If a certain mood state is prevailing, then particular coding and decoding processes are more active than others. For example, it is easy to generalize if we are depressed. In case we feel tired and frustrated, and our boss wants the best from us, we activate mental processes that are more on the "obsessive" tone, and the prevailing mental operations are those that allow an analytic thinking. In this case details and micro-information become relevant. We have also seen that the process of differentiation activates logical operations based on difference: "$\neq$". The opposite applies if we feel at the top, happy. Life seems wonderful and mental operations are now tuned on our "universal love". Practically speaking, we use more categories of thinking that allow a generalization, for example by using the summary thoughts Σ: anything can be put inside the same basket of flowers. To summarize these processes, I would propose to consider mind as an *amplifier*. As we have seen, once a certain affective state—depression, joy, obsession, etc.—is prevailing, it selects a specific category of ideas chosen from the many logical and mathematical processes we have met at the beginning of the book. Much more, these processes seem reinforcing the prevailing idea and mood, and each one reinforces the other: the affective state selects specific mental schemes, and these last reinforce the ideas on which that affective state is based. For example, if one person is hypochondriac, all the semantic information, the bodily discomfort, any change in the environment will reinforce the strength of the hypochondriac ideation. In other words, each input from environment will activate the prevailing set of hypochondriac thoughts. A small pain reinforces the false idea of having a disease, and this preoccupation selects specific cognitive scheme that will be used as a basis for that ideation: concentration is focused on bowel discomfort (activation of logic categories that elaborate differentiation), fear is exclusively based on the stress for medical check-up (activation of self-fulfillment prophecies), rumination is basically a recall of parents who suffered from life-threatening diseases (activation of old cognitive scheme), etc. The same happens if a person is mainly using an obsessive/ruminating ideation. Any change in the internal and external environment will influence rumination which is the prevailing set of that mind, and not the persecutory ideation, which here is less intense. It is like playing a tune on a triangle tuned in D minor. No matter how strong we hit the triangle, the sound coming from it will always be in D minor.

The same applies to a depressed person. He always responds to a "D minor tone", no matter how the inputs (keys played) arrive: social, biological, psychological, etc. However, it depends on how open the central *governor* (a synonym for "cybernetics") is, if a different tune can be played. By acting as a closed system (non influenced by inputs), mind works like a mechanical piano where the tune is automatic, the keys move by themselves, because the piano is reading an internal message made by a roll with holes, or like a carillon where a drum moves little pins of different lengths to make the same music. A carillon works as a closed system, its action is already determined by an internal *bios* with few chances to be modified. On the other hand, an open system is like a clever musician who is able to play any music according to the state of his soul and to the exigency of his program. A closed mind has already an internal program and shows rigid cognitive schemes. It always "plays the same music", with few chances to modify it, *unless* there will be an input able to act on the *bios*, on the program in order to tune it up. Psychotherapy and counseling usually act as external activators for different cognitive scheme. Psychotherapist, but also an empathic friend, helps the person in crisis to consider alternative point of views for problem solving.

This is conceptually and ethically important because a closed system is unable to adapt to the environment in order to make the right modification for survival. Any psychopathology leads to a lower adaptation of a person to any life stress or changing pattern because s/he is unable to modify the program of his/her mind, or to use successfully all the inputs and signals that derive from the environment. For example, s/he stays depressed and pessimistic in a party; the low self-esteem will lover fertility; the sense of guilt will enhance self-destructive behaviors; constant hypochondria will lead to excessive health expenses and to a life of poor quality.

If a cognitive scheme is prevailing, it is possible that a person is using some mental operations that are more frequent than others. And we have already met them: *and, or, if then, more, less*, etc. Prevailing cognitive schemes are self-reinforced because mind will select input data that strengthen the running mental process. When we are depressed and low spirited, we use absolute categories, and if "anything seems always so sad" it is because we have our attention focused on sad events while we discharge what is happier. If we feel happy and elated, we seldom select a calm music. Self-reinforcement also is a result of specific behaviors that feed the prevailing cognitive scheme. The weakness of a depressed person makes him/her feel less willing to start sports and, therefore, there is a positive feedback that self-feeds weakness. Final result is that by avoiding a stimulating a social environment, this person fails to be exposed to different inputs. At the end, generalization appears and things really "seem always the same".

The hypothetical circle of self-reinforcement is:

Affective state ↔ Cognitive category

Affective state ↔ Selected environmental stimuli ↔ Activation of specific thought processes

For the expert scientist the question of *reversible causes* is always present. Is a person depressed because s/he does not find friends or, vice versa, this person does not find friends because depressed? Is the happy person elated because s/he has many friends, or s/he has many friends because looks happy and elated. And, finally three questions: 1) Do we feel depressed because we think with depressed cognitive schemes? Or, 2) Do we think with depressed cognitive schemes because we feel depressed? Or, even more, 3) Do depressive schemes and affective states have similar causes responsible at the same time for "feeling" and "thoughts" that are depressed, elated, and obsessive, etc.? In my opinion, nowadays, science is accepting more multi-factorial explanations and the hypothesis that affective and thought processes are simultaneously generated from multiple environmental, biological, physical, social, and genetic causes.

Finally, in order to close this chapter, it would be preferable to talk more about *psycho-openness* and *psycho-closeness*. In this last case, as it could be during strong emotional states, crises, losses, our mind is basically focused on its own operations (*and, or, if then*) lazy to respond to external changes, allied to the same coping strategies, and little influenced by any mutation in the environment. During psycho-closeness, and in any closed system, mind acts always according to its internal program no matter how different the inputs are. The risk is to waste all psychic energy to self-maintain deviation or poor mental operations (*and, or, if then*) until no energy is left to a person to interact with the environment. From an outsider's point of view, the way in which this people behave seems highly biased and not "open" to constructive changes. At this point, only external and decisive interventions either on the cognitive scheme (i.e., cognitive-behavioral therapies) or the affective state (i.e., psychotherapy) can bring to a condition of psycho-openness and to effective strategies for problem solving. At times, self-healing in resilient people ensues, and this reminds us about the strong potential that our mind has for insight and self-cure. A slight modification in feelings or thoughts has been able to trigger a cascade of healthy processes that bring our mind back to more effective thought processes. Considering that our brain is highly sensitive to the biology of our body and to environmental factors, it is enough to normalize, for example, the glycemia with insulin in order to go back to a feeling of well-being.

5.6. Mind as an encoding-decoding machine

Data used to build the theories reported, mainly were gathered by using the semantic content of the problems reported by people, by using *words*. That is, the information about mind and its processes were collected by considering the amount of information contained in the verbal material (*semantic* content of the message). The idea of self and others, the idea about reality, all expressed by words, were the data I worked on. Communication theory is helpful when we can characterize mind acting as an *encoding-decoding machine*. That is, mind elaborates inputs from environment as messages and after encoding/decoding processes, it transforms them in ideas (thought processes and problem-solving strategies), and sensations (what we feel with our senses: vision, smell, hearing, taste). No matter how different the inputs are (verbal and non verbal messages from others, data from our physical environment, reactions from our body metabolism, etc.), we always transform these data in ideas, and these are usually expressed to others by words. Also if we do not talk about what we think and how we feel, our internal dialogue is based on a flow of verbal expressions (a sort of internal running commentary) assembled by the categories of formal logic. An example? I am feeling happy and I tell to myself: "I feel happy when it is sunny". I have used an *if-then* ($\supset$) category for assembling internal data: "*If* it is sunny *then* I feel ...!". The semantic content of internal and external communication, our words, our ideas, are assembled by logic connectives (*and, or, if then,* etc.) as the pearls by a nylon thread.

In a clinical setting, one way our analyst has to assess how we feel, and how/ what we think is by addressing us some common and polite questions: "How do you feel? What do you think about others and the world?". If the counselor or clinical psychologist has a good training, he can understand if we feel depressed, anxious, obsessed, by deciding what logic connectives are prevailing in our descriptions. Are we generalizing? Are we jumping to conclusions without a proper exam of reality? Are we poor in coping strategies? We show these emotions by expressing specific ideas characterized by some cognitive scheme. Cognitive psychology has plenty of data about these schemes. What is new is that cognitive schemes do use recursive logic connectives and mathematical operations (seen at the beginning of this book) to cluster ideas. In some extent, there would be no cognitive scheme without basic logic connectives, and there would be no personality without a prevailing cognitive scheme. The smaller is the number of logic connectives used to assemble our ideas, the higher the chances of biased ideas. To a certain extent biased ideas can lead, during pathological mental states, to overvalued ideas and delusions. But also staying in a normal setting, mind can alternatively act as an open or closed system (using systemic terms) depending on the use of selected or expanded mental operations (logic connectives).

It would be helpful to recall that in any closed system, entropy increases spontaneously while information decreases, the same way in which entropy is a measure of disorder, of chaos, while information a measure of order, as Wiener suggested[16]. For example, under stress and strong emotional turmoil, we are focused on a small array of information and ideas. If I have been fired, I can hardly think about other matters. All my attention is focused on the job I have recently lost, and as a consequence, information available to form other ideas decrease in number. If this goes on, there is a progressive loss of problem-solving strategies, because these last need a certain stock of new fresh ideas in order to help us coping with the loss. The final result is that the more we are focused on that problem (loss of job) the lower are the chances to restore mature problem solving strategies. In the cases where the feeling of loss and sorrow is longer, we assist to a progressive apathy and "laziness" in idea formation. That person is in the point of no return, and clear thinking might be jeopardized for ever. Now the chances of becoming mildly or severely depressed are very high. If this person meets a close friend, this last can get the impression that his depressed friend has a "fixed idea", and is generalizing his loss by using absolute categories when he states: "I will not find another job in my life. The world has no place for me. There is nothing else to do". What emerges is that these messages lack of semantic complexity, are simplified, and do not consider as true all alternatives. That is, there is a lack of information about reality. To make another example that can illustrate a biased thought, we cannot convince the hypochondriac that his chest pain is not a tumor. He is not able to enclose in his system of beliefs all alternatives linked to a chest pain: heart neurosis, stomach gas, stress, etc. Therefore the information "chest pain = cancer" is semantically of inferior quality than the information enclosing all alternatives for a chest pain. In addition, biased ideas self-maintain this restricted complexity by considering as real only one of infinite alternatives. In addition, alternative information coming from environment and others (that should act as neutral stimuli), will instead work to feed that pathological ideation. Not only is pain considered to be cancer, but also whispering amongst doctors talking in front of the patient is taken as proof of this preoccupation ("They do not want to scare me!"). Finally, also changes in body homeostasis (temperature, bowel movements, etc.) are interpreted (decoded) in the same fashion.

To summarize, any psychopathology or a biased ideation has the following characteristics:

- Mind is acting as a relatively *closed system* with an increase of internal entropy. Practically it is not amenable to change by external feedbacks, information, and ideas.

- Mind shows *a semantically poor ideation*. The analysis of mental codes, of logic connectives, of the "thread" that links ideas, show that this person is not using the same complexity we have found in the Renaissance Man. We witness a restricted use of mental categories and connections, even if ideas seem many and "creative".

- *Mind self-maintains its status*. Any alternative message or idea coming from others or environment is always decoded and accepted according to the basic assumptions of the system (depressed ideation, paranoiac ideation, delusional ideation). A depressed person selects from the world stimuli, ideas, and conducts that reinforce the prevailing cognitive and emotional state. A depressed executive always "finds" news about companies found in bankruptcy. A depressed youngster always selects books and music with sad stories.

- There is *little success in changing the system from outside* (psychotherapy, psychoactive drugs, resetting the internal clock, changing the social environment, etc.) unless these efforts are directed to the cofactors of pathological ideation or to the basis of cognitive schemes: i.e., the serotoninergic pathways during depression, degrees of humidity and temperature for environmental stress, food quality during malnutrition, etc.

- *Self-healing is always possible* and successful as long as there is insight of the prevailing cognitive scheme and its change in more successful thought processes.

From here, some interesting conclusions. We can still act on the entropy of the system if we are able to select the proper input to send to the system. In addition, mind should be considered as a complex system which needs different categories of inputs (social, psychological, spiritual, and biological) in order to create unbiased thoughts and understandable cognitive schemes. A person has a natural tendency to complexity, and, because reductionism is not the proper way to consider the wonders of mind processes, we should pay respect to the complexity of human mind to the point that a multisciplinary approach is needed either to treat or to describe thought processes. Thoughts are affected and can be influenced by a complexity of inputs. The final cerebral pacemaker will then make a sort of average of all inputs by selecting an answer, in this case, an idea or a cognitive scheme. This last is the end result of an arithmetic mean of "all" incoming stimuli: social, biological, physiological, neurological, environmental, and spiritual. If I am feeling happy now, it is not only because I won a bet, but also because I have no hypoglycemia which would lover my happiness, no invading neighbors that use my swimming pool when I am away, no spiritual dilemmas, and no threatening environment. Having a "happy" cognitive scheme is a result of complexity. And in some sense I agree with those who read some of these pages who commented that I have a "complicated mind". I prefer complexity to reductionism! Victor Frankl[17] calls people who want to look for simplified solutions and explanations as *terribles semplificateurs*.

As a result, *the Logic System of Interpretation (LSI) will determine the way in which mind treats concepts and inputs coming from the biological (body), psychological self, others, and spiritual environment.* Usually, in the *semplifier*, mind treats environmental complexity by transforming inputs into a set of limited ideas and schemes. On the other hand, in the *analytical* person, complexity in incoming stimuli is maintained and multiple logic connectives (*and, or, if then,* and others) are activated in order to produce ideas with a high complexity and containing a lot of information. According to cybernetics, as long as an increased complexity of the living system is assured, life can continue, and the system will survive. According to system theory, this is accompanied by a decrease in entropy.

5.7. The cybernetic diagnosis and "psycho*logics*"

The aim of cybernetics and system theories has always been the introduction of unitary models. Up to now, we were able to approximate the end output of a course of actions, or mental operations, when the inputs and their signs were known. In its basic assumption "Cybernetics is the study of regulation and control in systems, with emphasis on the nature of feedback" (Rollo Handy and Paul Kurts, 1964, cited in Littlejohn SW, 1983)[18]. However, with the use of logic symbolism we may soon predict, by knowing the output and the input feedbacks, the *logic of the system* involved: mental processes. Therefore, by knowing the quality of the inputs and the logic of the system we can predict the output. That is, by knowing what kind of data our mind is elaborating (losses, stress, high blood sugar, low protein intake, etc.) we can predict our emotions and behaviors.

Finally, by knowing the output we might predict a set of inputs and the possible logic of the system. That is, when we discover that a friend is depressed (mental output) we enquire about causes (inputs) asking if some loss, has occurred, if s/he is eating well, if s/he has been fired, ect. This is shown in the following case study and in the figure below.

If we translate this to our daily encounters, we have some chance to understand interpersonal relations. For example, if I know that a nice woman likes flowers, and that she is happy when she receives them, then by buying flowers for her anniversary (input), and by knowing that she is usually happy when she receives flowers (logic of the system), then I can easily predict that she will be happy and grateful (output) if I buy her a bush of flowers. I will now talk about a person I met during sections of daily counseling. This example will help us to understand how our nice logical and mathematical expressions can be easily applied in a clinical setting.

Daniela is an 18-year-old woman who has been suffering for years of fluctuating psychosomatic symptoms (headaches and stomach ache) which have not found any relief from treatment. At the interview with her parents it emerged a conflicting relationship between her mother (that Daniela considered very close, understanding and affective), and her father (described as an obsessive and possessive man, unable to show loving feelings). Daniela is unable to express her anger, and all negative and unexpressed feelings make her feel always on the edge, and unable to be optimist. Although an antidepressant therapy was started, she made no improvement in her low self-esteem and pessimism about future. In addition, a basic narcissistic personality emerged. She felt very important to be considered "a pretty and a good girl". In her social interactions, she was not developing mature strategies, and she was always seeking approval from others. In addition, she felt unsafe in the world. In fact, she was not able to make autonomous decisions from her parents' guidance, and felt the world as being unsafe and the people as being all untrustworthy and critical, like her father was. As a consequence, by feeling world and people as rejecting she could not develop a mature autonomy in order to depart from her family nucleus still considered as "safe", even supposing the conflicting relationship between her mother and her father. In some sense, she was generalizing and projecting the rejecting attitudes of her parents onto other people. She was "generalizing".

Generalization, as we have seen before, is a known cognitive process during some emotional experiences. During depression, we use a part of our experience to make inferences about the whole picture. We feel sad because we might think that the whole world is the same, for example full of people who do not like us.

Therefore, what we find during generalization is a general statement that embodies a premise (part A) and a general conclusion (Part B). More simple statements inclusive of a subject+verb+adjective contain little information about that person. For example, the statement "I feel unhappy", does not tell us why and when. Therefore, during psychotherapy the analyst always ask for further information about that simplified statement. When some more complexity is achieved in the statement of a client, we proceed in the analysis of how bit of information are chained together. In the example reported below, statements are linked by connectives like "when" and "because".

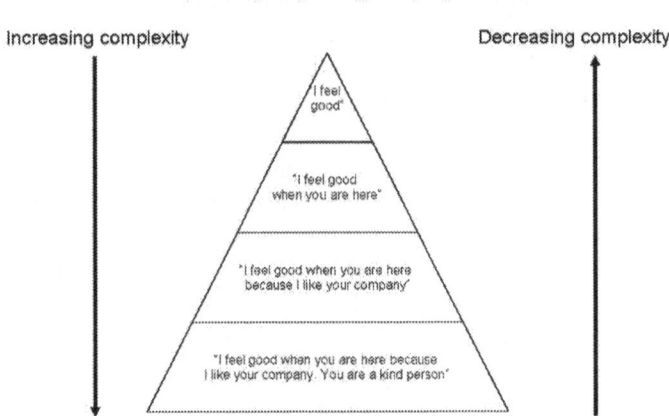

The psychotherapists who wants to make a clinical diagnosis, usually focuses on inner experiences of his/her clients "usually" reported as verbal statements. The analysis of the elements that belong to these assertions—and how nouns, verbs, adverbs and adjectives are arranged inside these statements—is a powerful tool for detecting ideas, feelings and emotions of that person. Usually, statements bringing important information and carrying an acceptable level of complexity, can tell us the prevailing mood state, or, if the analyst is well trained, can suggest a probable psychological diagnosis: depression, paranoia, mania, compulsive disorder, etc. Again, the most valuable parts of these statements are the *connectives* (*and, or, if then, therefore,* etc.) that link the parts inside the whole statement. Sometimes, in a simple schematic analysis, statements can be divided into two parts, A and B. A is the antecedent, usually the personal experience telling how that person is feeling and what is thinking, while B represents the part supporting and justifying what is stated in A. The parts A and B are usually linked by logic connectives, and the choice on how linking A and B depends on the prevailing ideas about self and others that that person holds. For example the statement "My friend does not like me, *therefore* people do not like me too" is suggestive of a generalization. The therapeutic effort of the analysis is to transform the connective "therefore", and to question the part B "People do not like me too". Statements are not always this simple, but an initial explanation can help to cope with the analysis of more complex statements. For example, a statement can be composed by several parts (A, B, C, D) each one linked to others by logic connectives. For example, we can find a structure of the kind: i) if A then B; ii) If A, then B and C; iii) A, B therefore C, etc. Logic connectives are helpful to everyone to create ideas and to make a decision. These connections are used in our daily life and not always are they pathological. For example, "Rains, therefore I need an umbrella" is a brilliant idea while "If it rains then I feel very depressed" should raise some suspect.

Other times, the first part of the statement is meant to identify one's personal experience, i.e., a sad family environment during childhood. The second part of the statement could refer to a more general experience drawn from daily life. In this case, if we translate this thought into symbolic expression, we have the first part of the statement (part A) indicated by p and the second part (B) by q. When we deal with psychological transference the p statement usually refers to the archaic o early experience which influences all the following experiences q. In the symbolic representation of statements, we will use the sign "~" indicating a negation of each statement, either p ($\sim p$: read: "non p") or q ($\sim q$: read: "non q"). Let us stay with statements suggesting a psychological transference. In these statements, we make some kind of generalization where, personal and narrow experiences will narrow a wider perspective about truth. For example, if we had a bad experience with dogs, and were attacked by a dog when we were children, it is possible, when adults, to have some extended phobia about dogs. We will always consider them at risk for assaulting us, even though we never let them come close. We feel that all dogs are aggressive and could assault us. Perhaps, inside the statements and justification we make of our phobia, we have some *p-q* statement where we justify our fear of dogs because of that unique episode in childhood when we were assaulted by dogs. But dogs can also be friendly; they help blind people, and are good companions for lone people. However, no matter how, our first contact with dogs, *p*, will generate a sort of explanation, *q*, using a logical connective of the kind if-then "⊃". The final idea is that: "If that dog has assaulted me, then any dog can assault me". The stronger that experience of assault the higher the chance of considering true the statement *if-p-then-q*. Usually, our early life experiences increase the likelihood to find *if-then* statements to any following similar experience, given any proof that there is no link between the two. In our life we are somehow flooded by *if-then* statements, strongly held, that can open a way to biased ideas. Usually, we use or "transfer" a portion of experience to general categories, and a part is used to identify the whole. In addition, if the first experience with a part, *p*, was accompanied by a high emotional state, then that part *p* is taken as indicative of the whole *q*. That dog that scared me will generate in me the basic idea about dogs in general. "If that dog was nasty, then each dog is nasty". Adopting a more objective look about dogs, would decrease the occurrence of transfer ideas, and *if-then* statements of this kind. Usually it is possible to identify, four categories of *if-then generalizations* according to the characteristics of the *antecedent p and consequent q*:

1. *Form particular to general*: *p* refers to a specific member of a category, while *q* refers to the whole category. For example I knew a nice cat when I was young, and after that moment I liked all cats that I consider as nice as the one I knew first. *If p then q*: if that cat was nice then all cats will be nice.

2. *From general to particular*: *p* refers to a large category, while *q* refers to a specific member of a category. For example, while I was on the mountains, I collected eatable and tasty nuts in the wood. Now I have an unknown nut in my hands, and I suspect that this also is delicious. Perhaps this is not true, and that I cannot eat that nut because poisonous.

3. *From particular to particular*: *p* refers to a specific member of a category, and *q* too. When I was in my holydays abroad, I met I nice old lady in a bakery. I though that all old ladies serving at bakeries are sweet. Now, I am in a new bakery, and an old lady is serving me. I am encouraged to share my feelings because I think she is like the first one I met during holydays.

4. *From general to general*: *p* refers to a large category, and *q* refers too. When I was abroad, in a country, I met many nice people living there. Then, I moved in another country and, before meeting local natives, I thought that they were nice as well.

All these categories can be at risk for biased thought, because they do not help us to analysis and to fine discrimination. They are all OK, but at times, it is important for us to make some important distinction that would help in coping with the bulk of data that come from our environment. Our personality has a role in deciding which link is better. If I am positive and open minded I choose to see anyone as friendly, also people that I do not know well. If I had a painful experience during childhood, whatever reminds me that is categorized as "equal" to that experience even if not. Other times, it is our emotional arousal or our needs that decide what kind of link shall be selected for joining two apparently similar experiences: p and q. The effectiveness of these links or transference depends on what I am dealing with. Knowing that all rattle snakes are poisonous because I knew one poisonous rattle snake in the desert, will keep me away from them for ever: "If one is poisonous then all are poisonous". Wishes are also strong selectors of the categories of generalization. If I am thirsty and I am dying to drink fresh lemonade, any glass with a yellow liquid inside and ice is almost confused with lemonade, also if it is sulfuric acid.

In case of danger, we find almost similar processes. Our attention is narrowed, and we estimate as similar, things that are not. Again: *a strong emotional state will narrow our point of view and will make us generalize inputs from the world.* If I meet a cobra in the desert, and I am running away from it because scared, I may interpret as a cobra any think moving in the bush or even a black rope. In this case, generalization $p \cong q$ has saved my life. Therefore, in any state of alert, we are drawn to generalize and to make inputs look similar. This mechanism could help us to save our life. But in other circumstance, we must learn to make differences, and generalization $p \cong q$ is no longer fit for our life.

This is what happens during negative emotional experiences in life, and if $p \cong q$ was a way to adapt to a violent environment during childhood ("My father was nasty therefore also other men are"), this must be modified during the late stages of life even by psychotherapy, showing that there could be no link, and that the interpretation is that there is p and q and that they are separated. In therapy, the effort is to link predicates by the conjunction "and" where different experiences are kept isolated in order to treat data without using transference mechanisms: *if p then q* $(p \supset q)$ shall be changed in *p and q* $(p \wedge q)$, that is, "My father was nasty *and* other people are not nasty". When generalization is no longer acting, people can think independently and inputs, statements, experiences, can live autonomously, even if there are some similarities, as it follows.

In the following examples, I have reported some categories of common generalizations and the circumstances where they mostly appear:

1. *Generalization*
   - If $p \supset q$: "My father is/was *good*, therefore all men are good"
   - If p is true $\supset q$ is true: If may *father* was good so are all men; If it is true that my father was good then it is also true all men are good.

   Or

   - If $\sim p \supset \sim q$: My father was not good then all men are not good.

2. *State of alert during danger and healthy generalization*
   - $p \cong q \cong r \cong s$: I am running *away* from a cobra, and I think that a slight movement in the bush could be another cobra.

3. *State of generalization because of activation of emotional arousal, sad recalls and experiences:*
   - $p = q = r = s$. Susan has been victim of a violent father. She reports her emotional experience stated as a theory about people: "My father (p) was violent with me, which means that other men (q) are also violent. From here I assume that it is normal that my boyfriend (r) is violent to me, as any other man would be (s)".

When we go back to the case study of Daniela, we find that she has developed, about her world view, a system of interpretation of the kind $p \supset q$. That is, family upbringing and education, conflicts between parents, plus her obsessive and possessive father have shaped her system of interpretation towards selected logic models: "I cannot trust my father therefore, I cannot trust people!". This basic script makes also the target of therapeutic interventions. Daniela acts as a closed system, but Daniela is brilliant and still able to make a reality test. Her cognition is not impaired although depressed. However, a mood style, thus a psychological substrate, is enough to influence some assumptions about self and others. Consequently, she will consider as false the following hypotheses that are contrary to her basic cognitive schemes about men: $p \supset q$ = *nasty father $\supset$ nasty men*:

i)   that her father is nasty but that other men are good ($p \wedge \sim q$);

ii) that her father is good and that men are nasty ($\sim p \wedge q$);

iii) that both her father and men are good and reliable ($\sim p \wedge \sim q$).

Daniela seems generalizing her father's characteristic by projecting his critical attitude onto any other male figure. Therefore, the case of Daniela, as that of other young people with similar histories, seems to suggest that behavioral experiences would make us to treat environmental inputs according to our inner Logic System of Interpretation (LSI).

In case of organic pathologies of brain, or even pathological emotional states deriving from altered physiological parameters (high blood pressure, low or high blood sugar, low blood oxygen, cerebral dementia), these connectives show a particular rigidity, and the whole experiential world, including dreams, assumes selected aspects: anything seems gloomy, threatening, etc.[19]. In this case DSM-IV-R manual suggests to talk about "*organic personality*". Basically, all reactions, emotions, stable behaviors that resemble a personality trait can be impaired by an underlying organic change of the body physiology: i.e., altered blood levels of any substance, viral or bacterial infections, blood pressure or hearth rate, food, vitamin deficiency, etc. A differential diagnosis from functional personality is important in order to save the life of people who, sometimes, seem suddenly changed and assume unexplainable behaviors.[20] For the same reason, by offering the right biochemical inputs to body (protein, vitamins, low food sugar, etc.) it would be possible to enhance personal feelings of well-being.

Black box theory, makes assumptions about the logic in the system by knowing its outputs (behaviors, personal statements), and by knowing the inputs (*p and q*) ($p \wedge q$). This is the same strategy used for psychological diagnosis.

As first conclusion, deriving form clinical observations, we consider as "parasitic thoughts" (PT) those ideas felt as "true", although we can find few links or congruencies with the inputs that generated them. For example, if I am watching a paining, and I think "beautiful painting", the painting itself is generating a congruent thought, that is, it is creating a metal pictorial image which is "in tune" with the stimulus "painting". However, if the same painting, for example a landscape, generates a foreign idea, for example, "It reminds me my boss", this "parasitic thought", showing low congruence with the generating stimulus, is inhibiting the generation of a more realistic thought and idea. This PT does not belong to the expected results of seeing a painted landscape. A PT is a sort of inhibiting stimulus of more congruent thoughts CT.

Therefore, anytime we have, for example, two inputs, one being a parasitic thought (*pt*) and the other being a congruent thought (*ct*), the final mental idea depends on what is prevailing between the two thoughts. Biased ideas are the end result of the prevalence of parasitic thoughts over congruent thought: $pt > ct$. On the other hand, unbiased ideas are the opposite: $ct > pt$.

If by looking a landscape a person comes with an idea which is scarcely linked to that painting ("It reminds me my boss"), then we arrive to the conclusion that a strong emotional state is acting as a parasitic thought, and that this one is inhibiting the mental processes that, "at that moment" are trying to generate a more realistic idea: "It is a nice landscape". Usually any thought we generate is a dynamic process of reciprocal influences between parasitic and congruent thoughts. In a sense, we average thoughts that are closed to reality (congruent) with others that are very creative or foreign to the stimulus (parasitic). Consequently, the final thought or idea is *the best fit in a given moment and for a given condition*. I use the term "best fit" in order to avoid the mistake of talking about "truth" which has little sense in cognition and mind processes. On the other hand, *best fit* much resembles a process that helps us to generate *thoughts that help us to survive, and to solve problems*. At this point, we can assume that congruent thoughts help us in the development of the *best idea, which helps us to solve problems* (psychological, social, behavioral, emotional, physical, etc.). On the other hand, parasitic or biased thoughts *do not help us to solve problems, or can even make problem unsolvable* (like a chronic depressive ideation, or a morbid obsessive rumination). As I have said, I am talking about average of thoughts (best fit + low fit) because even in conditions of pathological thoughts, people have residual stocks of best-fit ideas that can reinforce in order to move to healing or to a better interpretation of reality. In this case, we are much closer to a *gradient of fit*, a sort of summatory process of best-fit and low-fit mental processes, because the whole process is dynamic, and not fixed as could appear by using a rigid diagnosis. In order to give a final version by using our beloved mathematical expressions (one more does not harm!) I shall try to write:

Survival ← best-fit ideas outnumber low-fit ideas
Survival ← Sum of best-fit ideas > Sum of low-fit ideas
Survival ← Σ best-fit ideas > Σ low-fit ideas

$$S = \Sigma b > \Sigma l$$

Or alternatively

$$S \leftarrow \Sigma b$$

With this last expression we simply understand that the survival of a system, (biological, human, and social) is determined by the number of best-fit ideas, that is, *ideas that let the system survive*. In other words, there are no "good" or "bad" ideas, mental processes, economic strategies, or psychotherapies. We should verify if the array of mental processes proposed by a theory helps a person or a group to cope with reality, and to solve personal and interpersonal problem. If yes, then, those mental processes are probably in the category best-fit. On the other hand, if a person sees that personal strategies, that are "always" result of mental processes, are creating more problems, then it means that the ideas that s/he is using (any idea or thinking, as we have seen, being the result of emotions and environment) need revision, even if they seem good. For example, some people suffering of low assertiveness are always kind with others. Being kind to anyone is ethically right, but does not help that person to survive. In fact, s/he suffers because has no boundaries. Even being nasty to anyone is not the best fit. The antisocial adolescent does not face feelings of guilt but the fear of being arrested or bullied by peers. Therefore, antisocial behavior is not helping that adolescent to survive.

5.8. Mastering world complexity

We know from mathematics that aggregates or sets form unitary wholes characterized by certain characteristics, and that relationships amongst aggregates are defined by functions. In addition, relations amongst aggregates substitute relations amongst systems where feedbacks are functions that link the member of one aggregate to the other. A sub-aggregate, therefore, represents a subsystem. Watzlawick in "Pragmatic of Human Communication" says that the paradigm of simmetry-complementariety is that which is closer to the mathematical concept of function.

To make an example John and Karol love each other. John feels that his life would be empty without the existence of Karol. John is functioning according to Karol existence; therefore, John is a function of Karol. Karol and Mary are sisters, and belong to the set of Karol's family, while John is Susan's son, and they make another set or family. In the following figure two families, that had no bonds, are now linked by the love of John for Karol.

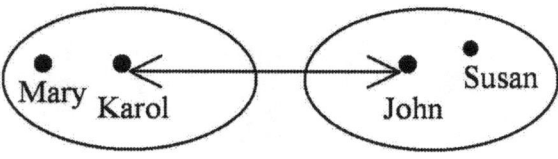

$$J = f(K)$$

(Read: John J is a function of Karol K)

$$K = f^{-1}(J)$$

[Read: Karol K is an inverse function of John J]

In a similar way, our mind links different ideas that belong to different sets. It can make leaves a function of trees ($L = fT$), and trees a function of vegetables ($T = fV$), etc. Moreover, mind functions as a system which elaborates inputs on the basis of its LSI in order to determine the output or thoughts. Inputs are information from the environment (social, psychological, physical) while the only outputs a mind is able to produce are thoughts or ideas (or behaviors as a consequence of those thoughts). For example, when I see a fresco painted by Michelangelo, I feel happy. Here a visual stimulation as determined an idea of happiness. But also when I can get some fresh air in a hot summer, my mind generates ideas of happiness. Finally, when I spend some time with my friends, I feel content. In the three examples, physical or social inputs are transformed into ideas. Pathological thought disorders, in some circumstances, are a deviation from these schemes, and social, psychological, and environmental stimuli generate exaggerate responses that are somehow unexpected compared to the incoming stimuli.

I have chosen to consider mental operations applied to inputs to generate outputs as similar to the mathematical concept of "function" f. Any function can be qualified as a transformation of an element a belonging (expressed by the sign $\in$) to the set or category A (for example, a rose belongs to the set flowers), into the output p (i.e., the thought "beautiful") belonging to another set B (i.e., category of esthetical ideas).

Fig. 5.8.1—As stated by Scorletti M, and Trioni M. I.,[21] we can imagine a function as a "box" which transforms an element of A (input) in an element of B (output). The concept box clearly resembles the concept of "black box" used by system scientists. The output "p" is a function of the input "a".

$$[a \in A]_{input} \to mind = function\, f \to [p = f(a) \in B]_{output}$$

Here, some kind of interesting transformations that our mid is able to do. As a clever magician what goes inside the magic hat, mind, is transformed in exciting ideas (Fig. 5.8.2., Fig. 5.8.3):

- An external physical input from environment is transformed into an idea or emotion. For example, any stimulation reaching our senses: i.e., light, temperature, taste, smell. For example, walking close to a fish restaurant the scent makes me feel hungry. My mind has transformed a physical stimulus reaching the organ of smell into an emotional state.

- A social input from environment is transformed into an idea or emotion. For example, the company of my college friends fills me with happiness.

- An internal psychological state is transformed into an emotion. I feel loved and cared, and I generate the thought of being at the centre of attention.
- An internal physical state is transformed into an emotion. A low blood sugar level makes me feel weak and low spirited.

Fig. 5.8.2.—Any input from environment is transformed into thoughts, y. These are the only outcomes of mental operations. If a, x, b are physical, social, and environmental inputs, they reach our mind by influencing our sensory organs (taste, smell, ear, touch) or our internal work stations (for example, feeling weak and low spirited when our blood sugar is low). It is important to tell that y, that is, thoughts, are a function of inputs (a, x, b) because of the transformation they receive in our working minds. The elaboration of inputs much depends on the LSI, Logic System of Interpretation which uses logic connectives to assist in the screening and elaboration of incoming stimuli. Mental operations, represented by the gray rectangle, are no more than the logic connectives we have seen along this book: _and, or, if then, therefore,_ etc. Incoming stimuli, often aggregate to generate a unique thought. In some sense our mind works in order to reduce world complexity. This can be the scheme of mental synthesis applied to a complex environment. We can also define this process as _convergent thinking_ manifested during synthesis and analysis.

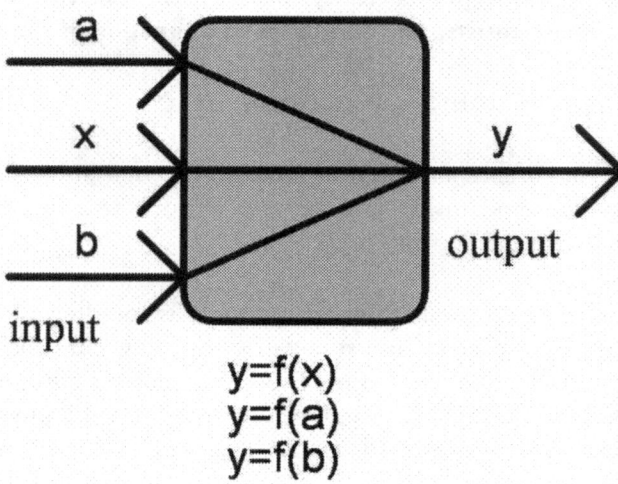

$$y=f(x)$$
$$y=f(a)$$
$$y=f(b)$$

Fig. 5.8.3.—Another attitude of our mind is that of being creative. We are somehow creators of meanings and thoughts, often starting from a simple stimulation. It happens during creative or *divergent thinking* when we have many thoughts and ideas just because we were looking at a masterpiece of art, for example, the Da Vinci Gioconda.

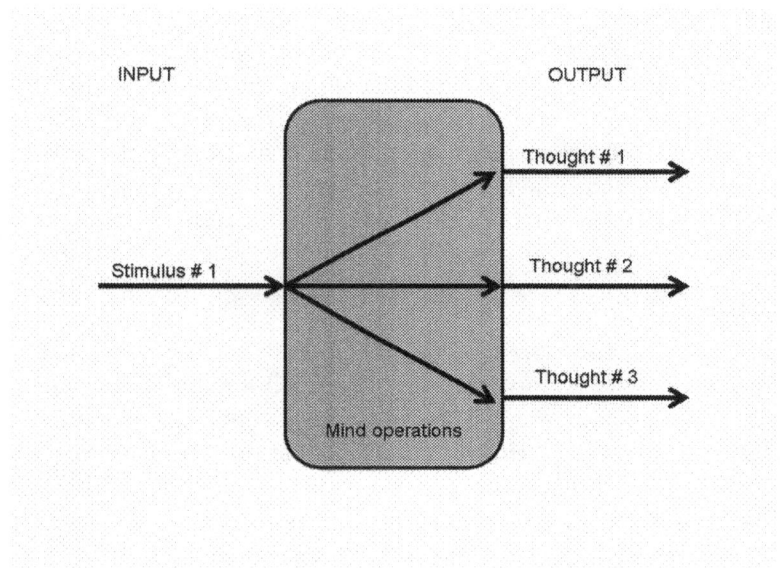

Pathological thoughts can be considered as an exaggeration of both processes of *convergent and divergent thinking* where there is an abnormal synthesis of complex environmental stimuli forming only one thought, or there is a burden of thoughts and ideas generated just from a simple input. In case of oversimplification, a person, no matter how complex the environment is, generates an omni comprehensive thought, for example, "I do not like anything in the world". In case of exaggerated divergent thinking that person is prompted to an infinite number of ideas by one simple input. These processes can also be seen in normal thinking. What changes in these circumstances, is the amount of poorness or richness in thought formation. Symbolically, in case of pathological convergence we have a person who is summing all incoming stimuli (x_n) towards a final thought (y):

$$\Sigma x_n \Rightarrow y$$

With $x_n = x_1, x_2, x_3, x_4, \ldots$

Otherwise, in case of exaggerated divergent thinking, ideas outnumber the inputs:

$$x \Rightarrow \Sigma y_n$$

with $y_n = y_1, y_2, y_3, y_4, \ldots$

One example of exaggerated convergent thought, is that of a depressed person who, when exposed to social, environmental and physiological stimuli, always thinks that the world is an "empty" place or that s/he feels empty. On the other hand, an exaggerated divergent thought is found in a manic person who, after having been exposed to a single stimulus, i.e. the picture of a rose, starts a train of thoughts about roses, beauty, life, philosophy, etc. Sometimes thought disorders are a consequence of mild or severe organic impairment of the organism or the brain. In this case, functional elaborations of inputs are strongly influenced by neurophysiology.[22]

Finally, we shall remember that there is no stable law for the transformations that mind can operate on inputs. Actually, we shall think that in a state of alert, and in few seconds, our mind is literally bombed by many incoming stimuli. Final ideas depend on the logic system operating at that moment, the number of stimuli that we chose to elaborate, and those we select for dismissal. Usually, both incoming stimuli and generated thoughts belong to specific sets, not always of the same kind. For example, if I see a rose, which is an entity belonging to the set flowers, I can have an esthetic idea or an inspiration for a panting, this belonging to the set "creative thoughts". The thoughts that we generate usually belong to some specific categories, with whom we are already familiar: esthetic thoughts, ethical thoughts, cognitive thoughts, emotional thoughts, etc. The same happens to incoming stimuli: biological inputs, social inputs, physiological inputs. For example, feeling muscular relaxation by concentrating on a painting is a physiological transformation (output) of an image (input). It is up to our mind the decision on how to gather stimuli, and where to position outputs, that is, in what category or sets.

Fig. 5.8.4.—Mind has the ability to select inputs, and to put them inside specific sets that not always match to the same sets of incoming stimuli.

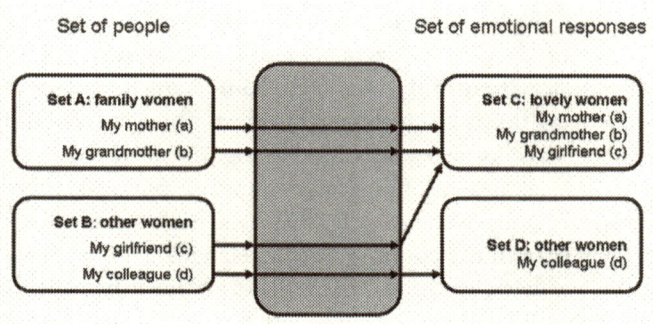

The symbolic representation of this selection would be:

$$[(a \wedge b) \in A] + [(b \wedge c) \in B] \Rightarrow [(a \wedge b \wedge c) \in C] + [d \in D]$$

Fig. 5.8.5.—Another example of mental selection.

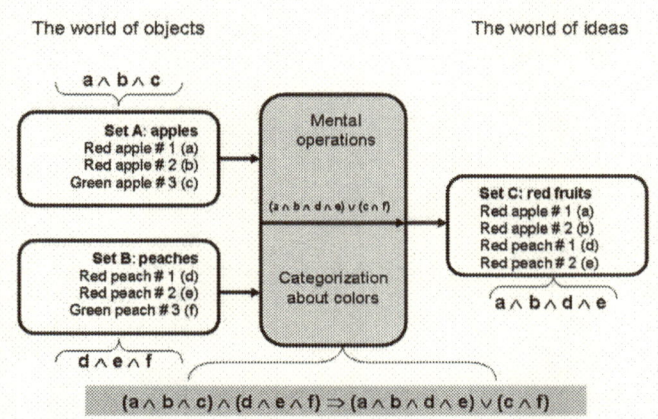

Mental operations and the working logic operations for incoming stimuli, sometimes require clustering into specific categories to the point that input clusters or sets, which generate inputs, and output clusters or sets, that generate outputs, are never equal. From here an important law: *mind operations are specifically based on the transformation of incoming stimuli, belonging to a category or set, into outputs or thoughts, belonging to a different category or set.* The emotion and its associated idea "beautiful" generated from seeing a flowers, is one of these example. Almost, any input is transformed to the point that mental operations are usually *set transformations*, categories that change into other categories. Having artistic, mystic, ethical and emotional responses to a physical stimulation of our eyes, for example just by watching the Sistina Chapel, can illustrate this idea. There is not mysticism in the painting of Michelangelo. Yet, we have transformed his paintings into esthetic emotions. All transformations that our mind presents, that is, our thoughts, all belong to abstract categories. Except from psychosomatic or behavioral transformation of emotions, whatever strikes our mind is transformed into an idea. In addition, categories of inputs are assembled or divided into our mind, using all logical operations we have met at the beginning (*and, or, if then*, etc.). This could give us the impression that these categories already exist. Yet, it is our mind that makes these selections, sometimes putting peers inside the basket of apples because it is using a categorization about colours, or flowers inside the basket or set of landscapes, because our mind is using a categorization about esthetical emotion.

Finally, we can say that also our emotions, the world of feelings, are the result of clustering of inputs inside specific sets of outputs.

Fig. 5.8.6.—Ideas are the result of transformations of inputs followed by the creation of other sets. In this case the number of output sets is lower than input sets.

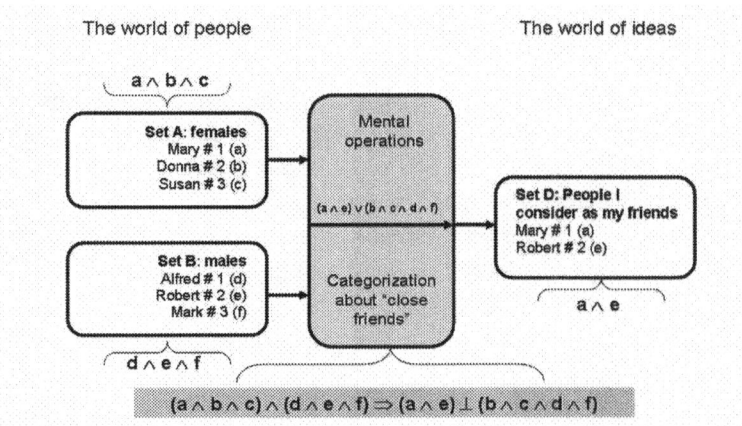

Fig. 5.8.7.—Elements of input sets can belong to many output sets. For example, "Mary" belonging to one input sets, in the world or ideas, belongs to two output sets. In this case there will be two mental transformations, #1 and # 2 represented in the gray lower part of the figure.

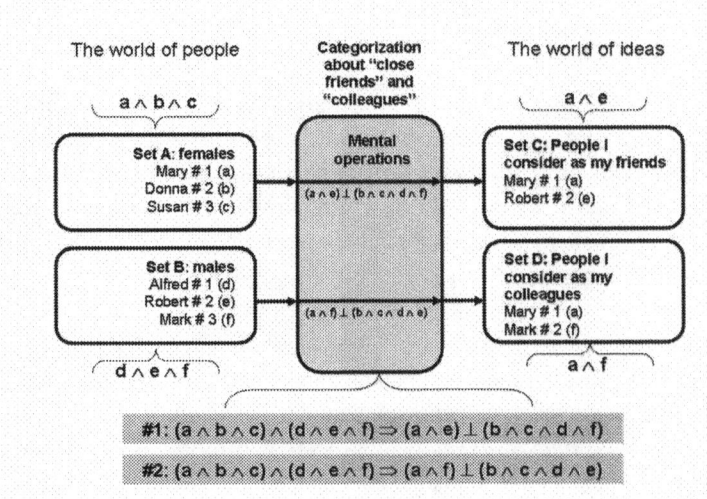

The way of clustering and creating output sets influences and is influenced by emotions. For example, a conflicting relationship of a person with his father would make him project this feeling also onto other fathers or male adults. On the other hand, the loving attitude of his mother would make him separate her behavior from that of fathers. Therefore, the psychology (LSI) of this patient will make him to put "fathers" and "my father" in the same set, while "my mother" in another one. However, this also happens during normal relationships where we aggregate people according to some core characteristics. In any case, we shall imagine a double route liking emotion to cognitive processes: emotions will elicit specific cognitive schemes which arrange inputs into specific aggregates, and, *vice versa*, specific cognitive schemes are responsible for peculiar emotions that select inputs according to specific clustering reinforcing those schemes. Or:

Thoughts ↔ Emotions

- Some examples in which clustering is at the basis of some attitudes (normal or morbid) are given by generalization, simplification, projection, etc.

- If a depressed person tends to generalize, s/he would project parental attitudes onto other adults, making them (inputs) similar in some way. On the other hand, an obsessive-compulsive person would consider any information different from others to the point that each one has its own salience and is highly different from others. Both generalization and subdivision are ways in which LSI interprets inputs. Changes are determined by psychological or organic causes. During a low activation of attention, differential stimuli are treated similarly. The opposite happens during high activation of attention, where fine discrimination is easier. Changes in attention, and in the process of "clustering" data, also depend on our psychophysical homeostasis: during anxiety we tend to be selective; during tiredness we loose fine discrimination and are more akin to make things quite similar (and when we are going to sleep all things seem so boring that we make our sleep a way of dreaming about a different world!).

People, objects, ideas, in the same aggregate are considered by our mind as sharing similar qualities. Therefore, if one statement is true for one member, then it is deemed to be true also for other members. By negating one statement about one member all members of the same aggregate will follow the same destiny. The logic connective which better explains this truth is *et, (and)*. The relation between two different aggregates, instead, is better characterized by the connective *vel* (*or*) where the truth is maintained even though one assumption is falsified. The scheme could be the following:

Personal statements:

1. "If my father (*f*) was a hard worker then all fathers (*f*ₙ) are hard workers".
2. "If my mother (*m*) was caring, then all mothers (*m*ₙ) are caring".
3. "My father (*f*) was not like my mother (*m*) [They are two different persons].
4. "Therefore, all fathers (*f*ₙ) are hard workers, and all mothers (*m*ₙ) that are caring"

Semi-schematic statements:	*Symbolic statements:*
If f then f_n	$f \supset f_n$
If m then m_n	$m \supset m_n$
$f \neq m$ (or: $f \perp m$)	$f \neq m$ (or: $f \perp m$)
Therefore, $f_n \neq m_n$ (or: $f \perp m$)	$\therefore f_n \neq m_n$ (or: $f_n \perp m_n$)

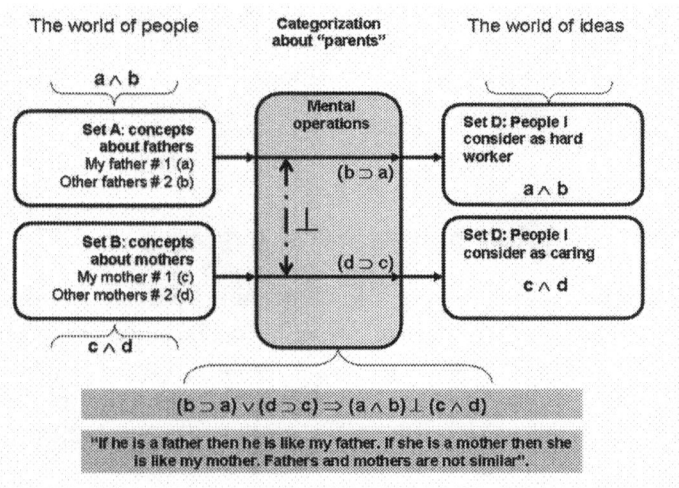

6   When our mind is in trouble

6.1. Introduction

Human and social systems have their own life! In this chapter, we will see that human and social systems share certain characteristics represented by crisis points, and the use of models to master environmental stimuli. When a system experiences a crisis point, there is a sudden interruption in its normal course. The system behaves in a complete different manner, unpredictable from its normal structure. It is "as if it became crazy". In this case, problem-solving is altered. The other aspect of systems is their tendency to use models to elaborate in the same manner discrepant stimuli from environment. Pathological human and social systems, instead, use different models of elaboration almost for each input. This is a prelude for increased internal entropy, and for a complicated way of system survival.

6.2. Unpredictable behaviors of systems

Not always, mind follows a linear and predictable behavior. In other words, system behavior, that is, the way men, societies, organizations react are non-linear and each time unpredictable. Predictability usually is not an appraisal we make on "actual" states, which could be normal and could run smoothly. Unpredictable behavior is something which belongs to living systems as well as to machines. Some assumption can thus be made:

- Systems display behaviors that are cyclic and unpredictable.
- What seems to be a non linear development of a back-and-forth quality is, indeed, a cyclic development that is always a linear and a forward movement (Fig. 6.2.1.):

Fig. 6.2.1—The projection of sequential points of a circle on its own diameter gives an apparent back-and-forth flow on the same diameter. However, the system "circle" is anyhow evolving and moving with no regression in its homeostasis.

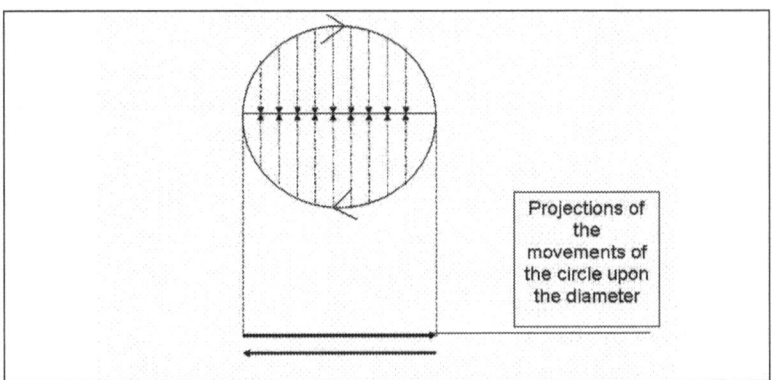

Projections of the movements of the circle upon the diameter

6.3. Crisis points

Our mind sometimes, shows *sudden and radical changes, stops, deviations,* to the point that it may or may not return to its initial status. Usually, there is a progression toward an inner state of entropy. We get the feeling to have changed, to be in point of inner turmoil. Sometimes we feel strange as if we had lost our sense of self and reached a point of no return. In a certain way, a **crisis point** (**CP**) is essentially unexplainable and sudden. Coming back to our assumptions, all systems show states of predictable and unpredictable behaviors, and mind itself, like any complex organization, shows these aspects.

Certainly we are not talking of changes like a reactive depression, because we have lost all our money in a web lottery. Really, the only assumption we can now make is that there seems to be nothing that justifies this sudden mental change.

Apart from an increase in internal entropy and disorder, sometimes, as a result of a CP, mind moves towards negative behaviors, social disorders, delusional thoughts, untreatable anxiety, etc. However, nothing can make us understand why this happens. In fact, *a crisis is sudden and unpredictable.* What follows are new ideas that could be creative, mystic, if the crisis is towards growth, or could be chaotic and disruptive, if a mental crisis is regressive. Sometimes, after a period of crisis our mind and thought regain the starting position.

Because human mind is the motor of any broader social and economic phenomena, after a crisis, human and social systems progress to an increased entropy, towards progressive disorder, destruction, death, mental deterioration, or, on the contrary, towards increased organization and development. etc. Human, social, and mechanical systems, all show a crisis point somehow along their own life. Mind, human beings, social systems all show crises points that *are aligned with the same processes that a single mind shows*. In other words, in order to understand social and organizational behaviors we shall refer to the basic unit representing the motor of these large behaviors: a single mind, otherwise, a single person. Only by interpreting the logical operations that a single human mind performs during normal life and crises points, we have a grasp of broader aspects of human life, and not vice versa. Therefore, a single mind with its basic mental operations, represent the map for interpreting man, society, and organizations. This process of *reduction to unity* simplifies the logic of broader social phenomena to the point that society and human organizations *somehow reflect in their behaviors* the basic mental processes of one single "standard mind". The model of "standard mind" is, more or less, given by the though processes explained in this book.

Another characteristic of a mental crisis is that it *generates from inside*. In other words, a CP does not depend on external inputs, otherwise we should talk about adaptation that is the hallmark of each open system. In addition, even a periodic check-up of the system, mind, and, in a broader sense, human organizations, etc., would not allow to guess when a CP it is approaching. In other words, there are no preambles neither alerting signals. Probably a CP is an internal and "natural" event which occurs as a developmental stage of a mind that grows anyhow. *It develops from inside the mind, the social system, the organization.* Where form? We do not know. Why sometimes we act strangely, as if we were no more the same persons? Why, at a certain point in our life, after a calm and organized life, we suddenly embrace a different world view? People's minds can react simultaneously, yet unpredictably, all at the same time, if these people are joined by some common quality, interest, and goal. Their minds seem synchronized to the point that, after a period of acquaintance, all mental schemes used for generating thoughts and ideas, seem presenting shared patterns. This is reported by many psychologists. However, how this can structurally happen is still a matter of debate. Consequently, by using my model I feel a profound respect for these processes that any time make mind not responding to reasonable predictions. The challenge is to explain in symbolic logic what a crisis is, and how several independent individuals can somehow share this delicate mental experience. Their minds have similar crises, at the same time and in a similar fashion. I feel that this spiritual aspect of thought process has open routes of investigations. I will make some attempt to approach it anyhow. Some assumptions to construct a model of a crisis are the following.

- We said that a CP acts as a sort of *mental pacemaker*. In some sense, it wraps and directs all existing mental and running operations and change the course of any action mind is taking. Therefore, a CP attracts as flower with the bees, the mental processes from one point on. This can be explained as: *if there is a CP (x) then anything happening in our mind (∀y) will be a function of CP (fCP)*, or:

$$\text{If CP then } \forall y = f(\text{CP})$$
$$\text{CP} \supset \forall y = f(\text{CP})$$
$$x \supset \forall y = f(x)$$

The only assumptions about a crisis point we can make are:

- A crisis point is a radical change of mental operations that are unpredictable and not preceded by alerting signals.
- It does not depend on external inputs, and, therefore, it is not an adaptation to environment.
- It develops from inside in an apparently functional and open system.
- It does not derive from increased entropy but could generate increased entropy.
- Empirically, the occurrence of a CP, although non predictable, is in relation with time T. I decided to assign the symbol Ω to the crisis point in order to recall that it is somehow linked to the end of a cycle and to the beginning of another. Therefore, it becomes the omega point somehow related to aging of the system:

$$CP \Leftarrow \Delta t$$
$$\Omega \Leftarrow \Delta t$$

In order to translate this expression into a symbolic logic we assume the following statement: Given enough time, any system will then present a process that we can call "crisis point" or "omega point".

This is the same:

$$\text{If } \Delta t \text{ then } \Omega$$

Or

$$\Delta t \supset \Omega$$

(With Δt any time elapsed from the birth of the system, or, in other words, it is the life of the system itself). Therefore, given enough time, any system will then present a process that we can call "crisis point" or "χ point". This is the same:

If Δt then χ

Or

$$\Delta t \supset \chi$$

- A CP could occur any moment during the life of a system. It is unpredictable and unexpected, while, time elapsing increases the likelihood of occurrence of one or several CP.

6.4. Other aspects of mental crises and behavioral changes

So far, we have seen that a mental crisis can have negative or positive consequences according to the new order of facts and ideas that mind reaches. Because we have tried to link human behavior to mental operations, the same we shall do in treating crises in a broader sense. Even when acting in group, our mind tends to be tuned and to be synchronized to other minds of our friends. Social phenomena are somehow a mirror of multiple mental operations performing similar tasks, or, in other words, using similar mental operations. But what happens in the group when one single subject (in the group) has a mental crisis? But also: "What are the next steps that mind follows after a personal crisis?". We shall try to answer in some respect to both of these questions because, somehow arbitrarily I have chosen, at this point of the book, to look at the *social mind*, which means, how our minds react with other people's minds, and what are our mental operations we share when staying in a group of peers. This is not always a matter of social psychology which tends to shed light upon reasons, behaviors, and emotions. In this book, core mental operations shall be used to explain social phenomena. Therefore, we can add the following comments to define mental crises.

During a mental crisis, *mental operations, and logic strategies are somehow subverted* to gain a new order of lower or superior complexity. For example, mind, which is at the basis of our emotions and thoughts, sometimes does its internal reset to generate alternative ideas and mental processes. We have seen that this mostly is independent from external influences, and this autonomous activity is simply linked to time. Which means, that only time passing would increase the probability of occurrence of crises. Otherwise, a mental crisis is unexpected and unexplainable.

After a CP, mind *will not follow linear behaviors anymore*, at least during the period when a CP is occurring. It is like telling that even mental operations and cognitive processes seem following fuzzy logic. Random assembling of thoughts, even if behavior is not much altered, is a sign of reorganization. Logic predicates sometimes also are reverted, and a person who was a generalizer becomes selective. On the other hand, someone who was scrupulous and linked to details, after a mental crisis shows generalization or different cognitive categories.

"Resonance" means that an idea, or a cognitive frame that was not in the repertory of that mind becomes prevalent. For example: a scrupulous businessman who, one day, decides to change market strategies and to invest in some project that was not in his mind before. The prevailing idea is that he does not want to follow the main stream anymore. His mind is sending signals that a complete and different strategy is what is needed for his business.

When we examine a system experiencing a CP, we do not find answers to the 5 basic questions: "what", "when", "why", "how", "who". We have seen that mental crises are unexplainable. However, this does not mean completely out of this world. It simply means that after a reset mind is able to use different mental strategies that were never used before, different problem solving patterns by using different logic predicates (*and, or, if then*). Also behaviors are affected. When I learned to do shopping in the supermarket, after a while I learned to read labels on cans, and to differentiate food that I was considering similar. Not any cheese is the same, and "Bread" is a broad category. But this insight just came in one day, while the day before I was still using generalization. Although learning has helped me, it is through a mental crisis that my mind refused to consider as similar apples of different origin. From there on, logic categories, applied to "apples" were less $a = b = c$ and more $a \neq b \neq c$. Basically, although behavior changes gradually, mental operations for radical behavioral changes adjust rapidly to a new world view. Therefore, *a mental crisis shall also be considered as the possibility to embrace a new world view, but also the beginning of psychological problems.* In my case, those apples are not all the same. This because logic operations are not gradual, and there is nothing between the sign "=" and the sign "≠", or any other.

After a mental crisis, mental operations car reach a *higher or lower degree of complexity*. In case of increased complexity, like it can be seen in children, the world of ideas becomes full of wonder, and the world of facts fool of magic. Life and its multiple facades assume an unexpected complexity which fills us of amazement. Our mental and logic operations become dynamic and open to a running adjustment and modification. For example, the apples I buy in the market, not only are they different, but are different in one or more categories: taste, color, smell, etc. The operation to indicate this dynamic state is the use of the Greek letter "delta" Δ which complements logic predicates. Therefore, a dynamic approach to apple differentiation becomes:

$$\Delta(a \neq b \neq c)$$

Not only are apples different, but their differentiation is a similarly complex process: one day I look for color, the day after for taste, etc. *In some sense, a change to higher complexity simply adds to our mental operations a dynamic change (in this case* Δ). How ever-changing our mind is! It follows that also our behaviors that respond to our cognitive processes, assume a higher degree of complexity. I will not be satisfied in simply buying apples from the basket. I want to smell them, to touch them, to look them. Again, although from an external observer, I demonstrated small behavioral changes in the supermarket, while choosing apples, my mind perhaps had already changed. There is a lapse of time from a mental change to an overt human behavior. This is why our brave businessman did not change his mind the day he made the total marketing change. His mind changed before!

After a mental crisis, a person would then: i) reach a new and stable normal status; ii) reach a lower level of complexity: for example, a person who was a creative worker after a crisis is no longer able to perform simple organizational tasks; iii) reach a higher level of complexity: any new creation and achievement could be thought to follow a mental reset; for example a person after a crisis seems being able to perform tasks of higher difficulty never done before.

A *mental crisis could be triggered by a subset of ideas that were not central up to that moment.* From this subset, this core idea extends to recruit other mental operations. For example, during delusional thoughts, there is a starting period where some ideas take a lead. A person feels that there is something strange in the glance of unknown people met on the road. Afterward, s/he might feel s/he is at the center of attention. A progression towards persecutory ideas depends on the force of recruitment of other ideas. The core idea "feeling at the centre of attention" can progress or not to persecutory ideas, while the idea "center of attention" is simply a subset of the whole ideas that person has had about world. Another example.

At the beginning of a passion, there is always a period of delicate feelings about a partner. Feelings of love, that can become a central mental operation, started as a cherished passion. Love itself was not the prevailing set of ideas of that person, because, perhaps, s/he was focusing on other things, like job, career, house, etc. In a certain way, the mental reset following a mental crisis shuffles the ideas, and gives the golden medal to a subset of ideas that were not the best choice at the beginning of the game. Social movements somehow parallel what happens in mind. The birth of a dictator and of a dictatorial government often shows a similar pattern. Indeed, the more a subset is discrepant from the organization of the whole system the more it is a "good candidate" to be a trigger for a mental/social crisis. Important cultural revolutions were born from "one person's mind" then, expanding by recruiting other people, states, systems, organizations. Therefore, in some extent, *a crisis point is the consequence of the action of an internal unit, subject, subsystem or subset of the whole system, organization, society. This firing sub-unit is somehow reacting to its own high discrepancy from the whole surrounding system to the point that it might take the lead.* If we examine in detail this statement we can make some assumptions by naming "*a*" this subunit:

$$\forall\, x \in U\!: f(x) = a$$

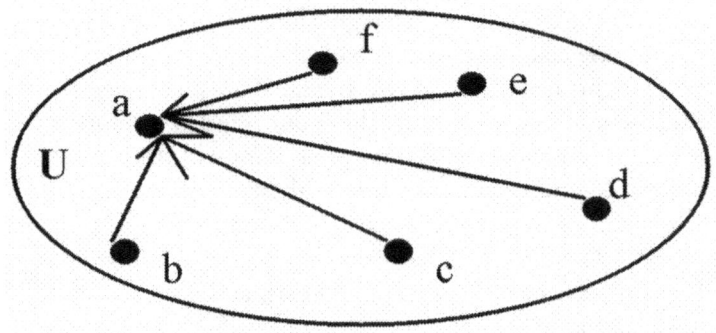

We can read this mathematical expression by saying that: whatever is the unit considered (in the set U the units are represented by letters *b, c, d, e, f,* which also represent ideas) belonging to the whole U, each one will convey towards *a*. Therefore, no matter how different ideas can be, they will converge to the prevailing idea generated as a result, or during, a mental crisis.

6.5. What happens during mental turmoil

People usually change because they feel that their ideas and cognitive schemes are no longer apt to face new incoming data. Therefore, a mental crisis can be a signal of an initial stage of change but also the state of a system that is trying new adaptations. Although our identity seems stable and constant, this is only a personal perception of what truly is a dynamic process. No core identity or knowledge we have is the same during time. There is always a variation Δ that accompanies the flow of identity and the flow of ideas. This is somehow different from what we read in some books, were there is the perception that we have one solid identity. In fact, the use of clinical and psychological classification for personality traits, or the custom to talk about self-esteem, low self-esteem, can hide the fact that these shall be treated as dynamic diagnosis and not immobile. We experience that our mood state change. One day we are depressed and the other day we feel elated. But also for personality we shall consider dynamic states. Feeling persecutory during periods of conflict with our boss. Or feeling obsessive when we are in the period of school exams. We find that emotions and thoughts shift on a continuum, changing in quality and intensity: more or less persecutory, more or less elated, more or less selective, more or less identified with our self. In some sense, mental turmoil is just the epiphenomenon or voice of this dynamic mental state. What counts in order to reach our sense of identity and stability is an *average* of all these changes. By averaging all our mood states during a twenty-four hour period we claim that we are basically happy or unhappy by the end of the day. For thoughts it is the same. We average the mental operations involved in mastering the flow of information reaching our mind. Therefore, the conclusion "apples are red" is somehow the average of all information we have about apples, colors, fruit, etc. Mental crisis, according to these new data we have about mind, is not much a sign of movement or change, but an effort to overcome stability and a status quo. There is a link between change, crisis, and growth to the point that development cannot occur without a crisis, and there is no change without a crisis. This is striking for business companies who fail to respond to market requirements in order to stick to their own mission and tradition. After a while that company no longer is able to respond to market.

Usually, our know-how, skills, and strategies are constantly challenged by new information and by the speed of environmental changes. If mind refrains from adapting to environment, then it sticks to a status quo no longer apt to respond to external data. Many business companies stay with their own old traditions, and sometimes they are unable to adapt to market changes and to environmental stimuli.

A changing and dynamic world is always forcing adaptation in our cognitive schemes and cognitive reservoirs. Sometimes mind adapts rapidly to changes. However, more rooted cognitive schemes, mostly linked to organize our sense of self, change less rapidly. We feel at ease when we change PC programs, and learn how to use new software for our work. At the same time, we do not feel comfortable to question our own sense of identity to make internal adjustments to change our stereotypes. During a mental reset there is a feeling of distress and crises because we are trying to readjust our cognitive processes. In a certain sense, a change in our deep cognitive schemes is the best mental strategy to cope with life, this processes going through mental crises.

Changing stereotypes and personal sense of identity, is not easy, also because this includes moving to reorganization in basic mental operations: we change our logic structures as well as related cognitive schemes (*and, or, if then*). Change is, thus, a matter of survival and mind sends us signals that mental operations that are familiar no longer are fit for adaptation to life. It sends us signals of the kind: "Or you change or you are in trouble". Even a change according to a law of convenience is acceptable.

Many organizations and business firm are adapting for their own convenience to the Chinese market philosophy, even though these organizations have not made radical changes in their own business philosophy. The same applies to many type-A personality people, who lower the level of their time pressure in order to reduce the level of anxiety and adrenaline. Therefore, if adaptation is a sort of reset of mental operations, of the kind we have seen at the beginning of the book, ways of adapting can be rapid or slow according to the complexity of mental operations employed. Some people change slowly because feel that they might have no cognitive skills to tackle certain tasks. Other people find this process easy. But, using a formal logic model we shall find that change Δ is somehow linked by time factor T to mental operations needed for change. In other words, apart from time, the speed of mental change reflects (is a function f) the complexity and number of mental operations (∂) needed to be changed:

$$\Delta = [f(\partial)] \, T$$

Changing frame of mind (Δ) is cognate to the complexity of the task ($f\partial$), and to time T passing in order to make a final decision. This is way we shall trust our partner when s/he tells us that s/he needs some extra time to dress for an important meeting or party. Mental selections of dresses require time T but also mental processes that help in the selection of the clothes, shoes, etc. But this process of selection can be seen as a little personal crisis, if the meeting is important, for example, it is a job interview. In this case, the final decision does not depend solely on the kind of dress to be used but also on other decisions, like matching the right dress for that interview. These processes are complex and this person, who is trying to look great for the interview is probably making some important decision for his/her life because that is the first job interview. We can predict a mental crisis, apart from stress and nervousness. Unfortunately we might give up changing our mind for tasks that are too difficult, for environmental challenges that we are unable to decipher or understand, and for life conditions that would challenge our sense of unity and stability. In some sense, we might try to determine when our mental operations give up change (Δ), and return to a previous level of organization or mental operations:

- *The task is deemed to be too difficult.*—We are convinced that we cannot grasp that complexity, and, therefore, we give up the analysis of the situation and the chance to adapt our mental operations. This is somehow at the basis of *voluntary illiteracy*. This represents a common human behavior when facing tasks that we considered too difficult to understand. Here, we stop mental operations and fail to adapt to the situation. For example, a child who has been convinced by parents that he will never succeed at school also during simple tasks, does not make any effort to master complexity and school requirements. The mental operation that stops change is:

$$\text{If complex, then no change}$$
$$\text{If } \partial \text{ then } \neg\Delta$$
$$\partial \supset \neg\Delta$$

- *The task is deemed to be too simple.*—Sometimes we feel lazy and tend to over simplify. Despite world complexity, we feel that we have enough mental strategies to cope with any problem. Some adolescent showing antisocial behaviors, when acting in gangs have the false perception of a magic power: they feel that there is no complexity or hurdle in the world that can stop them. Apart from being unaware of consequences for personal conduct, they reduce to unity what is plurality. In this case, change Δ in personal conduct and mental strategies fail to appear because a magic thought (which is a sort of defense mechanism) does not alert brain that there are failing mental strategies to cope with society. The symbolic transformation will be:

If simple (not complex), then no change

If ¬∂ then ¬Δ

$$\neg\partial \supset \neg\Delta$$

- *Mind has a false perception that there is no need for change because fails to register environmental threats or changes.*—Challenges to mental frames can come from outside, the world of facts, or from inside, the world of ideas. Sometimes mental adjustments needed to generate new fresh cognitive schemes, fail to appear because mind feels that there is nothing to be changed. Complexity of environment (∂) and the dynamic mutation of this complexity ($\Delta\partial$), either linked to the psychological or physical world, are not altering the brain. For example, a person is not alerted by the fact that s/he is becoming too aggressive and depressed. An adolescent fails to recognize that s/he is bullying school mates. A company is failing to adjust to clients needs. In these instances, there is no registration of complexity, and mind does not start mental operations in order to adapt to complexity:

$$\partial = 0 \supset \neg\Delta$$

6.6. Predictability, adaptation, and the use of models

What seems important in social behavior is finding reliable predictions about us, others, and the world. If things become predictable they also become reliable daily routines, and problem-solving strategies run smoothly. Everyday, we follow certain patterns of behavior. But we usually do the same things in a different way. Even if we have certain habits, and even if we do the same things at the same time, our actions are never the same. They are similar, but not the same. Therefore, we usually follow a *chain of actions, each action having its probability of occurrence.* Then, each behavior can be subdivided into other sub-actions each one having its probability of occurrence.

Our day is divided into some behaviors that, in a certain way, seem to be similar although they change enormously: waking up in the morning, saying something to our wife or husband, kissing our children, checking our mail box, getting on the bus, moving to our office. Although some behaviors seem to be always the same, they change enormously. In this case, *similarity* is only a matter of our perception: we do not kiss our children in the same way and with the same love; there is not always the same mail in our mail box; we do not take always the same bus; we do not do the same work each day. If each act is linked to a probability *p* of occurrence, a complex behavior should be imagined as a chain of actions, each one having its probability of occurrence. Therefore, "waking up in the morning" has its own $p1$, "kissing our children" $p2$, "taking the bus" $p3$, etc. We will consider possible implications in a while.

Let us say that mind always tries to *reduce complexity*, in other words, it applies interchangeable models to elaborate data. Our understanding of the world cannot imply the use of different models for each input we are exposed to. In some case, our methodology to understand the world and its endless discrepancy is to apply few cognitive models in order to reduce complexity into simplification. Categories, for example, will make it easier to understand a certain characteristic of an animal species. Through the use of social models, we can predict the behaviour of complex human organizations. By using some familiar adjectives ("tense", "down", "low spirited", "happy", "at the top") we simplify our diagnostic check-up or our mood state.

As a consequence, in order to simplify the world, we must learn models, and we must learn how to create models. Models are basic mental operations or strategies used to master different tasks. Therefore models help us to survive in a dynamic and rapidly changing world. Even a habit, a behavior, a personality can be treated as models that help us to face all-changing situations (the world of data). The way we kiss our children or the way we work is a model. *If we express this concept by using an empirical formula, we can assume that a model (μ) is a way of treating different variables as if they were similar variables, with each model representing a cognitive strategy to cope with different data (problems, environmental stimuli, needs, crises, etc.).* At this point an algebraic expression could be:

$$\mu \supset \forall x \Rightarrow \exists' y$$

The expression is read as: "If we use a model μ, then (⊃)we will treat all variables x representing external data ($\forall x$), by using only one cognitive strategy y ($\exists' y$).

Keeping the world and its inputs the more simple we can is a matter of survival. Simple systems, like cells, or complex systems like human organizations, cannot afford to change rapidly and deeply. *Adaptability of systems to life is somehow linked to their way to apply a model in order to master a changing environment.* Many systems cannot adapt (remain "closed") because they have no models to apply, or because they apply models in a highly diversified way, such as, to almost each input. According to this last conduct, each input, event, fact becomes salient to the point that even mental operations could be altered. Categorization or simplification, instead, would allow an easy adaptation of mind to incoming data, by simply using models. What happens when we are applying diversified models to all incoming data? Let us see.

- A model μ will be applied to each life event (loss, marriage, and crisis) ε_n, resulting in differentiated behavioral reactions β_n.

- Any life event will generate cognitive schemes or models μ_n of analysis: $\mu_n\varepsilon_n$. Each, cognitive scheme resulting in a different behavior or idea.

- During an overload of life events, the use of multiple cognitive strategies of coping will determine a mental overload and an emotional stress

- While in a normal condition, we use almost similar cognitive schemes or models to treat similar life events, during psychological crises and mental overload, we use different models μ_n for similar events ε as if they were multiple ε_n.

- In a normal mental state, while facing life events that are similar and that show higher probabilities of occurrence, mind tries to use the same cognitive models μ to generate similar behaviors. For example, in this case, there will be less cognitive mental schemes for opening doors, if the doors are always the same.

In a normal state, if complexity ∂ tends to decrease, also cognitive schemes or models μ tend to decrease for similar behaviors ε.

$$\text{If } \partial \Rightarrow 0 \text{ then } \mu_n\varepsilon_n \Rightarrow \mu\varepsilon$$
$$\partial \Rightarrow 0 \supset \mu_n\varepsilon_n \Rightarrow \mu\varepsilon$$

However, during mental crises we find the opposite. The inverse of the *reductio ad unum*, reduction to unity. Several life events, somehow similar, activate different cognitive schemes which generate different behaviors to cope with those life events. The loss of self-esteem will cause a complex elaboration of stimuli to the point that each stimulus is considered salient, unique, and complex, that is, different from others. We may say that this person lacks in adaptation. For a very depressed person it is difficult to perform simple actions, and there is an attempt to use many cognitive schemes and ideas to master simple tasks:

$$\mu\varepsilon \Rightarrow \mu_n\varepsilon_n \Rightarrow \partial$$

This, in the extended form is:

If ε_1 then μ_1, or if ε_2 then μ_2, or if ε_3 then μ_3, or if ε_4 then μ_4

Or:

$$(\varepsilon_1 \supset \mu_1) \lor (\varepsilon_2 \supset \mu_2) \lor (\varepsilon_3 \supset \mu_3) \lor (\varepsilon_4 \supset \mu_4)$$

If we call with $n\varepsilon$ the number of events occurring and $n\mu$ the number of cognitive models mind applies to master those events, the break-drown of the system (man, organization, business, etc.) occurs when:

$$n\varepsilon \equiv n\mu$$
Or
$$\forall n\varepsilon \Rightarrow \exists n\mu$$

{"Whatever is the number of life events $n\varepsilon$, we find a corresponding number of cognitive models $n\mu$ to cope with those life events"}
Or
$$\forall \varepsilon \Rightarrow \exists \mu$$

{"For each life event ε exists one and only one mental strategy or model μ to cope with it"}

In conclusion, each time a system (mind, human organizations, and living organisms) adapts to the environment it will use a model which is applicable to different inputs, each one characterized by a resulting behavior. In addition, *adaptation through the use of a model (or cognitive strategy) is a way in which mind and social systems survive to an all-changing external environment. As a consequence, highly pathological human and social systems use a large amount of models to adapt to external inputs. Some people show clear efforts to learn new complex models to master almost any slight change in the environment. To them reality seems always unknown and unreliable mostly because they strive to treat any input by using new cognitive schemes.* People showing high levels of anxiety, have high cerebral arousal and alerting states because unable to recognize repetitive patterns to each new stimuli. They seem unable to match new stimuli to old recollections. Everything seems frightening because it appears "so different" from what that person already knows.

In some business organizations, there are managers who demand from their subordinates different strategies to master familiar problems. Their subordinates feel unable to master their apparently new tasks, and a conflict could appear: "Now they tell me to do so. The day after, to do in a different way. I do not know anymore what to do!". Human beings react in the same way. Under a certain internal or external pressure and stress, given enough time, a life crisis is characterized by the fact that a person is not able to generalize events and, by feeling endangered by new life events, is now using new cognitive models when there is no need. In this case, a person becomes highly influenced and overwhelmed by secondary details. As a consequence, s/he finds difficult to adapt because s/he is trying to cope with each event in a different way. S/he is facing each one at the time.

Adaptation is therefore a way of making good guesses (that is, inferences about probabilities of occurrence) about changing environmental stimuli. Therefore, adaptation of a system is not just a matter of a response on the spot, that is, at the moment when an input occurs. Indeed, this is the behavior of systems "at risk" that is, those that treat environment as unreliable. The loss of adaptation in human and social systems is followed by the application of numerous cognitive models for mastering repetitive data. There is a limited number of models a human or social system could apply. However, the number of models, in a well working system should always be minor to that of the events. But when they are similar the entropy of the system increases and its life is endangered. It would be like using one and only one antibiotic for each different bacterium, like preparing organizational goals by training each worker in a personal manner, like changing our skills each time we face a problem in our work, like meeting the world as if previous experiences and knowledge about the world were useless.

6.7. Human beings and their uniqueness

The uniqueness of any human being should always be underlined. We also feel that some emotional answers are more predictable and stereotypical when compared to the infinite number of inputs that any person receives during life. However, within some range of mistakes, it is always possible to construct a map (usually identified as categories) of personality traits because we show similarities in behaviors, thoughts and cognitive processes. But if our minds are different and unique, how would it be possible to construct psychological categories and diagnosis? Well. Our minds are not similar, while we process inputs and data using specific categories of logic. In addition, no matter how different the inputs are (neurochemical, social, psychological, physiological, environmental), final mental "outputs" are always thoughts and cognitive schemes that trigger certain behaviors.

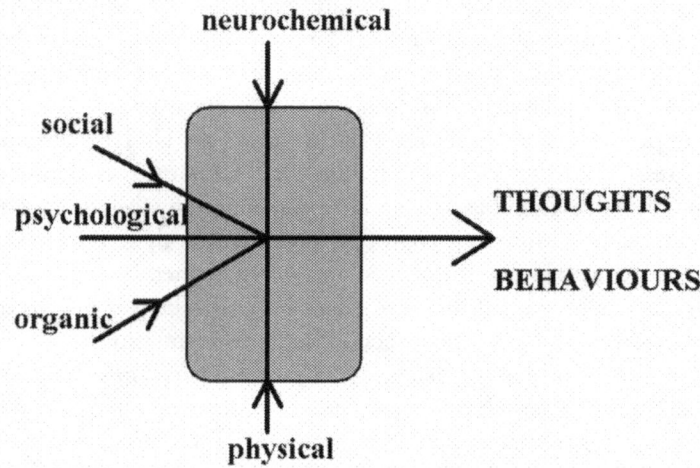

Many studies have confirmed this assertion, and this starts to become a stand point of any social discipline: human psychology, affection, emotions, even personality are the end result of an array of different inputs. Mind is a sort of transformer that generates *monomorphic outputs* (thoughts, ideas, and feelings) *from polymorphic inputs* (social, psychological, organic). Outputs are thoughts and ideas, while inputs anything affecting brain.

Thinking is the average process determined by tuning the several instruments that use our mind to generate the final music: social, organic, psychological, physical, etc. We can divide these influences as internal to our body or organic (I), such us, blood pressure, physical fatigue, level of blood glucose, level of blood iron, etc., and external (E) or psychological, such as any psychological experience, social changes, family factors, work pressure, level of social support, etc. Each of these factors will develop specific emotional reactions and cognitive appraisals, independently and accordingly to the amount of its influence. For example, a painful loss is much more influent than a slight variation in blood sugar. This allows a range of feelings and emotions related to that loss. However, even a chronic hypoglycemia can generate strong feelings and emotions. As we have seen before, our mind *averages all multiform inputs in order to determine specific homogenous outputs: namely thoughts and behaviours.*

Therefore, as in any social and psychological change, we shall imagine a threshold level instead of a direct effect. This last would implicate that we should see psychological and important changes since the beginning of a change in Internal or External Factors. I feel that this would make our thoughts sensitive even to a slight wind stream. Instead, the existence of a threshold implicates a change after our mind has performed an amount x of mental operations on incoming stimuli. For example, if we have a number n of internal factors I, and a number p of external factors E that we think might influence thought formation, we should assume a consistent emotional and cognitive reaction after a significant increase Δ in the value of internal and external factors. That is:

$$\text{Tought Change} \Leftarrow \Delta \ (nI+pE)$$

$$\tau \Leftarrow \Delta \ (nI+pE)$$

The value (nI+pE) can be measured and it represents the arithmetic mean score of the scores that can be attributed to each event by the person itself. A self-appraisal is important in determining the impact that each internal and external event has on one's own life.

External factors could be any life event as it is measured by many psychological scales dealing with losses. Internal factors are any event as it could be inferred by variation in internal biochemical and neuroendocrine parameters. We shall arrive to use the same scale dealing with amounts of changes. With more research we can better define the units used. For now, we can approximate by using scores.

Tab. 6.7.1.—Measuring a probability of thought change following internal and external factors. Each change gets and "arbitrary" score from 1 (less severe change) to 5 (more severe change).

Event and time of occurrence	Scoring	Total scoring (self-appraisal)
External		
1st	Loss of job	5
2nd	Changing home	4
3rd	Dealing with a temporary low income	4
4th	Breaking the car shift	2
Internal		
5th	Rise of diastolic blood pressure	4
6th	Hyperglycemia	4
7th	Milk intolerance	5
8th	Influentia	3
Total score		31
Δ(nI+pE) = Mean of 31 =		3,582089552

Only life events that score 4 or 5 usually result in changing mental operations, and affect emotions and thoughts. That is only for $\Delta(nI+pE) \cong 4$ or 5.

Basically, our brain elaborates these different inputs or life events, in the same fashion, first transforming these experiences into neuronal excitation (ON) or rest (OFF), and then selecting a set of cognitive schemes that, taken together in a certain way, output the resulting emotion: i.e., depression, anxiety, excitement. Thus, if we both feel depressed (output) it means that the set of cognitive operations (or subsystems) that generate the feelings: "feeling down", "being pessimistic", "having a low self-esteem", and so on. Saying the same into logic statements, it means that the system mind is "tuned" according to a certain set of possibilities in examining "statements" from reality. This set corresponds to almost any of the expressions in symbolic logic [∧ (et), ∨ (vel), ⊃ (if then), etc.].

Table 6.7.2—Theories on cognitive and behavioral processes in mind

Postulates	*Proofs*
There is not such a thing like one "hard" character, personality, or feelings. Persons are *psycho-dynamical* and not *psycho-static*.	People change in their feelings daily "although" what one person is or feels represents an "average" of his/her usual feelings.
Psycho-pathology is a trend towards a *psycho-static* mind.	People with psychological troubles, show prevailing mental operations that do not change easily, although data from environment has changed. For example, stay depressive even if a loss has been restored. Or still feel anxious after the end of a threat.
Identity is not much a matter of a static mind but is an average of our different selves. Our mental identity is a dynamic averaging of mood and personality states that also change dynamically, even in a short period of time. Personality traits and prevailing mood states are the final result of averaging mental states at the basis of personality and mood. The symbolic expression for change we used was Δ.	People continuously react to their environment (losses and gains), and without a basic substrate (core identity?) what we are at sunrise would not be the same at sunset. Personality, mood and thoughts are ways to *adapt* to internal or external environment. Even a persecutory ideation is a form of adaptation in a dangerous environment, and being lovable and accepting in a jungle is a risk for life. In order to adapt and to survive our mind selects a core of basic ideas that generate personality traits, mood, and affection.
In order to prompt certain behaviors and reactions we need adequate stimuli changing from one subject to the other. Circumstances and inputs that generate core ideas at the basis of personality, mood and affection, are not the same in each person.	Same (social, environmental, psychological) stimuli on different people yield different (behavioral, emotional) results. And if a threatening and violent city stimulates aggressiveness in some people, in others it could be the basis for a spiritual transformation.

Postulates	Proofs
There are people who react similarly to different stimuli: their inputs converge towards the same output (behavior, thought, decision, etc.). Their basic equation is similarity: $a = b = c = d = \dots$ n. Where a, b, c, d; are inputs. They simply generalize and simplify. They are *simplifiers*. For them, things cannot be contradictory. This could represent the best fit in a complex environment that changes continuously. Therefore, without simplification mind would be overloaded by data. In addition, from one statement these people usually predict the others. They use inferences based on partial assumptions: "If … then" "If John is young then John is inexpert". "If the city is violent then all cities are violent".	"Red apples (a), white peaches (p), green pears (g), red grape (r) are all the same. They are fruit". "I like fruit" "Therefore even thought I never ate green pears I feel that I will like them". $$a = p = g = r$$
There are people who react differently to several stimuli. Each environmental stimulus or input generates one and only one output (behavior, thought, idea, etc.). Their basic equation is: $a \neq b \neq c \neq d \neq \dots$ n. Where a, b, c, d are inputs. They make reality more complex. They are *analytical*. This could be the best fit in a predictable environment which does not change very often. More frequent in creative and analytic personality. From one statement they do not predict the others p ∨ q (p vel q): "John is very young or John is expert".	"John is very young or John is expert". Young *vel* Expert or (p *vel* q) or ($p \vee q$). However, John could be both young and expert.
One person could be a simplifier and an analytical according to circumstances, his mood state, and reaction to environment. Experience and memory could exert some effect. Simplification is a way of economically coping with reality and avoid mental overload. Cognitive complexity and deep analysis could lower an economic way of coping with reality but helps in tackling difficult and delicate tasks.	People who tend to simplify are more easily driven to make omission mistakes or to risk (lower selection of stimuli) ("they see the wood but not the tree"): *centrifugal thinking (from particular to general)*. People who tend to analyze are slower in data analysis and more easily driven to make mistakes in over-inclusion ("can't see the wood around the tree"): *centripetal thinking (from general to particulars)*.

6.8. Conclusions

To summarize, we have seen that human and social systems adapt to environment by making "good guesses" about the nature of incoming stimuli or inputs. In other words, they predict that certain events will occur or not on the basis of a certain probability. Even if those events will not occur, predicting certain inputs is at the basis for adaptation. In addition, events, either real or predicted, cannot be mastered by a step-by-step manner, that is by treating each one as highly distinct from other events or inputs. This would make the world unpredictable, and adaptation very hard. One way to overcome this obstacle is to use a model of behavior. As stated in this book, a model is an instrument that human and social systems use in order to treat several inputs in a similar fashion. However, pathological human and social systems loose this strategy. What happens is that each input is treated singularly, evaluated by its own cognitive model. But this way, entropy will increases and the system looses it capability to adapt to environment and to life.

7 Conclusions

In the book, we made an excursion inside the codes and schemes our mind uses in order to think. We know the efforts of making good guessing and the strain in solving complex problems. We also have experienced how difficult it could be thinking clearly when we are tired, anxious, hungry, or sleeping. Any second, in our life, our brain is literally bombarded by a bulk of inputs, information, chemicals from lungs or blood, nutrients and vitamins from gut, or carbodioxide in a crowded environment. These factors make clear thinking enhanced or impeded depending on the characteristic of these factors. Therefore, in a certain way, our process of problem solving is an average of 3 cooperating factors: i) internal environment: consists of emotions that facilitate or hinder thinking; ii) external environment: includes biochemical and bioumoral factors affecting neurons and cerebral centers; 3) the quality and quantity of the information or input that shall be elaborated by brain. The final thought, as we have seen, is always the final result of the combination of these factors.

In other parts of the book, we met very strange symbols that I have used to illustrate practically what happens in those few seconds when a mental thought is formed. I apologize if sometimes the description became complex, though with a second reading perhaps much more will become clear. I also want to apologize with neuroscientists that can righteously question the assumptions I made. Nevertheless, I feel that science is quite elastic and creative, and I have made some effort to enhance the beauty of mind and its processes.

From an ethical point of view I would like to stress that this book is an effort to construct a theoretical model, derived from a theoretical framework which borrows instruments from neuroscience, mathematics, formal logics, and cybernetics. However, these models are soon applied to practice, by observing how people think. Thoughts are explained not only in their "normal" functioning, but also in their "pathological" aspects.

Mostly, when I used models, I tried to figure out emotional and psychological situations that usually occur in daily life: anxiety, stress, depression, etc. Some hints are given also to thought processes in personality disorders, also to emphasize the continuum that any neuro-functional process presents within itself.

Finally, it has been highlighted the interpersonal aspect of thinking, as we live in a social context, and our thoughts and ideas are strictly interrelated with thoughts and ideas of other people.

Cybernetic and system models offer to many scientists some interesting keys to unusually interpret aspects of their daily scientific experiences, in this case, psychological, psychotherapeutic, and social. However, we should always keep in mind that the excitement of discovering new ways of interpreting phenomena through the use of inductive and theoretical research also creates many unexpected and unavoidable mistakes. Like in deductive research also theoretical inferences should undergone to replication and falsification approaches. In fact, there is not such a thing like a "true theory" but something which could help "practically" to solve complex problems. With the introduction of new technological instruments and knowledge, something could be added and something else rejected also in the assumptions made in this book.

8 Footnotes

[1] Thomson, R., Sluckin, W., "Cybernetics and Mental Functioning", *The British Journal for the Philosophical Science,* Vol. 4, N. 14, 1953.

[2] Perry R.B., "The Mind Within and the Mind Without", *The Journal of Philosophy, Psychology, and Scientific Methods,* Vol. VI, No. 7, 1909; p.169.

[3] Barret, C., "The Objectivity of Mind", The *Journal of Philosophy,* Vol XXXI, No. 7, March 29, 1934.

[4] Lazzari C., Lunardi A., De Ronchi D., Volterra V., Chiodo F., "Theoretical models for the explanation of impairments in the content of dreams (dream-phrenia) during cerebral pathologies linked to HIV". 4th National Congress of the Italian Society of Neurosciences, Pisa, Dec. 16-18, 1993.

[5] Lazzari C., De Ronchi D., Volterra V., Chiodo F., "Models for iconic thinking during organic impairments of CNS". 4th European Conference on Clinical Aspects and Treatment of HIV infection, Milan, Italy, March 16-18, 1994.

[6] Lazzari C., Campione F., Costigliola P., Ricchi E, Chiodo F., Dreams during brain atrophy in AIDS: a cybernetic neurophysiological model, 25th International Congress of Psychology, 19-24 July, 1992, Bruxelles. Proceedings published in the *International Journal of Psychology,* vol. 27 (3, 4), June/August 1992.

[7] Perry R. B., "The Hiddenness of The Mind", *The Journal of Philosophy, Psychology, and Scientific Method,* Vol. VI, No. 2, January 21, 1909.

[8] Falletta N., *Il libro dei* paradossi *[The Paradoxicon],* Longanesi, Milano, 1989.

[9] Wilkins, W. E., "The Concept of a Self-Fulfilling Prophecy", *Sociology of Education,* 1976, Vol. 49; 176-177.

[10] Henshel, R., "The boundary of the self-fulfilling prophecy and the dilemma of social prediction", *The British Journal of Sociology,* Vol 13, N. 4, 1982; 512.

[11]   Lazzari C., Costigliola P., Chiodo F., "A theoretical model of explanation of thought contents during HIV infection of the central nervous system: dominant clusters (DC), semantic clustering (SC), and cerebral pacemaker (CP)". Fourth European Conference on Clinical Aspects and Treatment of HIV infection, Milan (Italy), March 16-18, 1994.

[12]   Lunardi A., Lazzari C., De Ronchi D., Volterra V. Chiodo F., "A theoretical model for thought contents during organic personality and affective disorders". Personal communication, 16th Annual Meeting of the European Neuroscience Association, 18-21 September, 1993 Madrid, Proceedings in the *Supplement N. 6 of the European Journal of Neuroscience.*

[13]   Lazzari C., Lunardi A., De Ronchi D., Chiodo F., "A theoretical model for cognitive impairments during AIDS dementia complex". 4th National Congress of the Italian Society of Neurosciences, Pisa (Italy), Dec. 16-18, 1993.

[14]   Wiener N., *The human use of human beings.* Houghton Mifflin Company, Boston, 1950.

[15]   Kramer, P. *Listening to Prozac.* Penguin Books, 1993.

[16]   Wiener N., *The human use of human beings.* Houghton Mifflin Company, Boston, 1950.

[17]   Frankl V.E., *The Will to Meaning,* The New American Library, Inc., new York, N.Y., 1969.

[18]   Littlejohn S.W. (1983); *Theories of Human Communication,* Belmont, California, Wadsworth Publishing Company.

[19]   Lazzari C., Campione F., Costigliola P., Ricchi E., Chiodo F., "Dreams during brain atrophy in AIDS: a cybernetic-neurophysiological model". European Society for the Study of Cognition, Special Workshop: "Models of Cognitive Psychology"; Leuven, Belgium, 15-17 July, 1992 (Personal Communication).

[20]   Lazzari C., Chiodo F., "Organic personality and affective disorders during HIV infection of the central nervous system: theoretical models of explanation". Fourth European Conference on Clinical Aspects and Treatment of HIV Infection, Milan (Italy), March 16-18, 1994.

[21]   Scorletti M, Trioni M I (Eds.), *Sintesi Matematica* [Mathematics Summary], Vallardi, 1996.

[22]   Lazzari C., Costigliola P, Chiodo F. "Cybernetic and communication models for the explanation of loss of imagery and dream pathology during cerebral damages in AIDS", Fourth European Conference on Clinical Aspects and Treatment of HIV Infection, Milan (Italy), March 16-18, 1994.

978-0-595-45132-6
0-595-45132-2

www.ingramcontent.com/pod-product-compliance
Lightning Source LLC
Chambersburg PA
CBHW051442280526
45785CB00003B/1395